I Will
If You Won't Let Me

Kate Blake

ISBN: 9781726871167

ISBN-13

DEDICATION

I dedicate this to Clara.

Clara was the name I was given at birth before I was adopted. Since I saw my original name I've always felt a bit of double identity.

I am Kate Blake but if I had never been Clara I would never have become Kate.

CONTENTS

ACKNOWLEDGMENTS

I would like to start by acknowledging my Parents. All 4 of you. I do have a belief in a certain amount of Nature and Nurture, so I think I have to give you all credit for who I have become.

My Sons who have always been my inspiration and drive for everything I have done in my adult life. I have watched you have your ups and downs in life, but I am glad we have developed our relationship to a degree where we can lift each other out of any bad situations we may have got ourselves in.

My Daughter, I do hope your Mum is not too embarrassing. I love you to the moon and back.

My Husband, we work hard at things and if we continue to do so, things will be amazing. Thanks for your patience, I do appreciate it. My work drive and restfulness is hard to deal with I know.

My Brother who is always there even though we don't see as much as we should of each other and his family, who I hope will be more active in my life in the future.

My 3 sisters, I don't see you enough but enjoy your company so much.

I would like to thank lovely Lillian who helped me out when I needed help and has become the best of friends. Thanks for your support, we have lots more adventures to experience.

I thank Sarah and Lee for their years of friendships and memories of my Mum and Dad. You are as much family as you could ever be.

I would like to thank Andy C for giving me my first break in Sales and for laughing with me at the silly things in life. Tell Jules we are still overdue that coffee.

Shirley for being the best and bringing me tea and caring for me whilst I was going through losing my dad.

My colleagues and team mates now and over the years. We've had some amazing times and laughs, and you have been fantastic confidants in all my situations. I'm lucky to work in such a fantastic team.

James and Neal for believing in me and kicking my ass well out of my comfort Zone and making me stand up and talk in front of people, and for your support of me with this project.

Chloe, you are someone who revived my dream of helping women be successful. You will achieve great things. You already know that. I can learn a lot about how to shop from you, you know how helpless I am at that ha ha.

To Author and friend Christina Kelly for your inspiration in your writing of "The Secrets of Arran" such an enjoyable read. I would highly recommend it

Donna, Debbie and Kelly for being there for ages and loving my stupidity.

Mabs and Beryl thanks for your love and kindness.

Sarah S, we will be great business partners. We have an exciting future. So glad we rekindled our friendship.

Joanne and Kate I hope to be seeing more of you in the future as we are a big part of the past. It's been exciting to catch up. I look forward to our future.

To my longtime friends. We have had some big laughs in the past, we have drifted in and out of each other's lives but always manage to find our way back. You have all enriched my life. You will know who you are. Big Love.

Rob Moore, "The disruptive Entrepreneur" great podcasts and books.

And Steve Guest for getting me my first role in the Construction Industry.

Ange Loughran my Coach. Thank you for your support and I'm sure we will continue to work together, I'm not sure this would have happened without you. I am excited to see where this adventure will lead me next.

The Team at Authors and Co, thank you for making this happen for me.

1 Being Adopted, Early Family Life

I was born in Southampton in 1969 and due to my parents circumstances I was taken away from my mother at a week old and put up for adoption. I actually don't remember ever being told this, but I grew up always knowing this was the situation I was in.

What my mother did recently tell me is that when she was pregnant with me, the daughter of her Doctor who worked in London had asked her to participate in a book on Mothers that give up their Children for adoption.

She had declined as she didn't want people to know her business as things were much harder for Women in the 1960s. We said how funny that I would be the one of her children to write a book. Maybe I heard the conversation when she was carrying me.

I was taken to the National Children's home and must have stayed there for a while as my adoption papers actually said 1970, so it was perhaps six months before the paperwork was complete.

Obviously, there were no computers back then, so paperwork took time. I was adopted by two teachers who lived in Birmingham as an addition to their little family. They had already adopted my brother a few years previous. They were both in their 40's when they adopted us although had both been married for some time but not been able to have children of their own.

My father was a history teacher and my mother a reception teacher at a Catholic junior infant school. They were from the Methodist religion and lived a life around their teaching and Church social groups.

They were wonderful loving parents. We had a blessed and idyllic life. My brother and I talk quite often about the very fortunate situation we were in. We both know how fortunate we were to find ourselves in such a good situation. Our parents both really wanted children and would let us know how much they loved us regularly.

My father came from St. Austell in Cornwall and my mother from Dewsbury in Yorkshire. They Met in Birmingham when my Father moved to teach at George Dixon School and my mother's family were living there due to my grandpa's Accountancy work. He moved around a bit. They met at Sandon Road Methodist Church where my grandpa and nana and mum were very active church members and grandpa played the church organ and ran the musical events.

—

When they were married they lived in various bedsit type accommodations in Edgbaston but settled in Selly Oak, and later when they adopted me, moved to Devon Road in Smethwick by Warley woods. They purchased the house from a Psychiatrist who had been running his practice from there, and strangely enough this was the house my grandparents had lived in whilst they were in Birmingham, they had since moved to retire in Cleethorpes.

My brother and I were both adopted through the National Children's Home, my brother in 1967 and me in 1969. Both of us were from Southampton but from different parents. However, we were brother and sister as much as anyone could ever be. It seemed at the time there was quite a large amount of children in the adoption system at this time.

It was always odd to me and my brother that we both came from Southampton and we often wondered if we were actually really brother and sister by blood after all. It really made no difference to us anyway as we felt like a family and knew nothing different.

Our house was a villa type, 4 bedrooms with a living room, dining room and a large garden. It had white rendered walls, a small drive and front garden with a beautiful big cherry blossom tree on it.

Dad was a keen gardener, so the front garden and back garden was always well tended. Flower beds full of seasonal flowers, rose beds cared for and apple trees at the back of the garden having both eating and cooking apples. My mum used to make plenty of homemade apple pies from them.

Helping my Dad working in the Garden was great. We used to share half the neighbours garden too as they were elderly and couldn't manage the maintenance. Right at the top of our Garden by the fire pit there was a little gate Dad had made so he could easily gain entrance to this, and he grew vegetables sharing the harvest with our neighbours.

I would help him pick the beans, dig up the carrots and potatoes. Placing them in my wicker basket and proudly delivering them to our neighbours. They used to have two small dogs which used to chase and play with me for hours whilst dad worked hard.

Dad loved roses and we had a large part of the garden dedicated to them which he would tend with great pride. Red ones, yellow ones, white ones and pink ones. Mum would fill glass vases with roses and put them round the house and enjoy the fragrance, and I would make rose water out of the petals.

He always changed into his tatty gardening clothes which hung in his shed. A big brown cardigan which he would put on over a once good shirt and old suit trousers. Heavy brown shoes and wellingtons for wet weather.

It felt like a treat when he had a bonfire to get rid of any garden waste, he had built a big fire pit at the top of the garden surrounded by bricks which had been blackened by fire and time. In the early evening I would sit with him and watch the flames crackle and dance around whilst he stoked it and kept it alive.

We as children utilised the garden as much as we could, we had many summers playing out there, hide and seek, French cricket, spending time in our paddling pool with our friends from the neighbourhood. Running out of each other's houses, riding our bikes. We would make dens out of things we could find in the shed and the old coal shed which was used for storage.

The neighbourhood was fairly close knit so there was always someone watching out for us, and with that in mind we were generally well behaved. If anyone was naughty one of the mothers would have known very quickly. As with all childhood memories, looking back it seemed to always be summer.

My birthday was in June and mum used to focus my birthdays around the garden. One year we had quite a large group of my school friends' round and she did a lollipop treasure hunt and a picnic on the lawn after.

She had made one of her special chocolate cakes which we all enjoyed. Everyone had gone home with big smiles.

That evening when everyone had gone, there was a huge storm as the hot weather broke. I sat on the window ledge looking out of my bedroom thinking what a wonderful day it had been. Mum always was good at entertaining and put lots of effort into making my parties fabulous.

We had a huge tree in the middle of the garden which had a rope and a tyre to swing on and a ladder, so we could climb. One of our favourite pastimes was to put a paddling pool under the tree, fill it with water and swing across it on the rope. If you fell in you lost.

We would have a crowd of local kids all doing this for hours in the summer, drinking squash and eating cakes. Soaking wet running through the house with mum running after us with towels. We had tents, space hoppers, bikes and scooters. We were truly blessed. I felt very safe at home.

Sometimes though the thought that I wasn't really part of this did intrude into my nightmares, and at night from time to time, I did dream of unknown people taking me away from my safety.

As my parents were teachers they benefitted from having very long holidays. Their relatives were dotted all over the country which meant we were always enjoying visiting different places. Sometimes we would spend Christmas in Aberdovey in Wales where my uncle had a holiday home, New Year in Littlehampton where my auntie lived.

We would also take holidays in the Lake District, but my favourite was Gorran Haven in Cornwall. We would rent a cottage right on the beach and spend two or three weeks just relaxing and playing. We were lucky enough to be able to do lots of family things together either at home or away. My parents really prioritised their family time.

We were always very active but equally loved times in front of the television together. We used to watch a lot of comedy. We were a family with a good sense of humor and there was a lot of laughter in our house. The Two Ronnies, was a huge favorite with my dad, he loved the word play in the sketches.

They loved Morecambe and Wise and literally used to cry with laughter watching it. I used to worry that dad may have a heart attack and actually die laughing. I had once seen something on the news where someone had had a heart attack from laughing and used to worry terribly that this may happen to dad as he would go really red.

Strangely, I always thought Eric Morecambe was my biological dad. Obviously, he wasn't, I'm not really sure why I thought that, but I used to make up all sorts of potential biological parent stories in my head. When it's unknown, you can make your imagination run away with you.

Inspector Clouseau and the pink panther was a big favorite in the house. We loved Peter sellers and David Niven. Dad took me to the cinema to watch one of the Pink Panther movies.

Being the youngest in the family I obviously used to get sent to bed earlier than my brother. He got to watch Monty Python. I would sit on the Stairs and listen to the theme tune come on hoping I could catch a bit of what was going on, but it was never long before I was chased up to bed by Mum. I watched them all obviously at a later stage.

I have to say, as a family humor was a big part of our lives. We were taught not to take ourselves too seriously. That was a very good lesson.

Action films were a big favorite too and of course we all tuned into James Bond at Christmas, also The Great escape.

2 Nana and Grandpa on My Mums Side.

My mum's parents were lovely. They had moved to Cleethorpes into a lovely bungalow in the 1950s. We used to visit them regularly. Nana was so kind. She was very homely, and I remember she dressed very well. Always in matching clothes, accessories, hats and gloves.

She wore beautiful shoes. I was suffering from very bad eczema at the time and she had a wonderful silk sheet she used to put over me when I was particular itchy. I will talk more about my eczema later. Mum used to tell her not to spoil me. I think she just wanted to make me feel better and she did.

They had a white washed Bungalow in Aldridge Road in Cleethorpes near Grimsby. I never forgot the name of the road although it was so long ago. Funny how certain details stick in your head.

The bungalow seemed quite big from a child's perspective I guess and had underfloor heating. I would imagine this was unusual for the 1970s, but I used to love it as I always had cold feet. Grandpa loved gardening as much as my dad, so the front garden and back garden was always immaculate.

When we stayed over in the holidays, I mostly slept in my grandparents' room on a camp bed and my brother slept in grandpa's study where there was an occasional bed which was dressed in red silk sheets with a big red silk eiderdown. I remember thinking how luxurious it was and sounds quite gaudy now, but it was the 1970s.

He also had a big wooden desk where he did his work and in there he had wax and ink stamps to stamp on his correspondence. I would play at being a librarian with the stamps for hours.

Stamping bits of paper and placing the paper inside books and getting the adults to come and choose books and bring them back throughout the day. They were pretty good at entertaining my imagination and always would play along.

There was a little metal box on the bedside table on my nana's side of the bed where she used to keep blackberry pastels. I used to always sit on the side of the bed eating one after another, I didn't have much control when it came to sweet stuff. She didn't seem to mind too much though.

Grandpa used to use Brill cream in his hair, so they had to put lace doilies on the sofa to stop them getting oily. I'm presuming this was a regularity in the 1970s as I remember seeing this done on many people's sofas at the time.

False teeth were also something I got used to seeing at their bungalow. I think they both had them, because there was always a couple of containers with the teeth soaking in them in the bathroom every morning. I used to look at them with fascination. My Mum said I would have false teeth if I didn't brush mine properly and I certainly didn't want that, so I have always brushed my teeth well.

In the evening we used to get dressed up and go for a drive along the promenade to see the illuminations which weren't quite Blackpool, but everyone seemed to enjoy this ritual. Sometimes we were allowed to go in the penny arcade and spend some one pence's and half pence's. Nana would moan about grandpa's driving. I don't believe he ever passed his test but was given a licence after the war.

Cleethorpes also had a Zoo which we loved to visit, but bizarrely one year they took all the animals away, presumably a financial decision, and replaced them with plastic replicas renaming it the "Plastic Zoo". Strangely we still paid to go in.

We must have had time on our hands, but we really enjoyed it. Our parents would try and put us off as I'm sure they didn't enjoy it quite as much as we did.

There was also a big pool on the beach front made of concrete and painted blue where you could rent boats and ride around. I've got a picture of me and my brother in one of these boats. We loved that sort of thing.

We would get a present every week whilst we were in Cleethorpes for long periods of time. I remember my favourite being a doctor's case toy with which I used to run around insisting people were ill and try to fix them. I would sometimes get my grandpa to set up a tent, so I could have my patients line up outside for treatment.

I'm sure they were all thrilled. I think they would have much rather have been sitting in the living room listening to sport on the radio and reading the papers, but they played along graciously.

My memories of this time were so nice. One of my mum's relatives was a butcher and we spent lots of time with them. I think he was my mum's cousin. He was a character and always used to bring round great cuts of meat, but he also loved fishing so would bring trout for our dinner.

My brother enjoyed many fishing trips with him too. He smoked cigars and his wife smoked cigarettes in a long cigarette holder. She had tightly permed hair and was always smiling. Looking back now they were quite glamorous but unfortunately the smoke used to pay havoc with my asthma.

Relatives and friends of my mums' parents who we never saw again once the elders of the family had gone. They all came around to play card games on the pull-out green felt card table, the smell of cigars, whiskey and good food. My nana was a fantastic cook, main meals, lovely cakes and desserts.

We used to play "stop the Bus" and they used to let me win. I was sometimes allowed to drink a snowball and felt very grown up. I'm sure there are a lot of kids of the 1970s and 1980s who would share the memory of the snowball.

When it was bedtime, I would be sent to bed and there would be my parents, grandparents, uncles and aunties popping in to say goodnight before I would fall to sleep listening to the laughing and sounds of company. They were times when I felt totally safe and loved.

In 1976 we went up to see them in the 6 weeks holiday and stayed there for the whole 6 weeks. This was the year of the big drought, heat wave and infestation of ladybirds. Also, it was the year when my beloved nana died. At the time I didn't really understand as I was only 7, but I always wish she had stuck around longer.

Most of the time me and my brother were left alone, due to the grownups being at the hospital. We played hide and seek, I set up horse jumps in the garden and rode around on Grandpas walking sticks pretending they were my horses.

We made a large tent out of beech wind breakers and tarpaulin. My brother knocked my front two teeth out with a mallet by accident doing that. I was in the tent and he was going around the outside checking that all the pegs were in correctly, I put my head out from under the tent and he knocked my tooth out with a mallet. Nice. We weren't friends for quite a while after that.

My brother recently had one of the first reads of my book and pointed out the last bit about him knocking out my teeth was a little unfair and clearly, I had unresolved issues around this moment. History is always written by the victors he said. I will come clean on this and even the score in the name of fairness.

There was a time in our house when our dad had an array of truncheons for a policeman sketch he was doing for one of his concerts. Some were real and very heavy, and some were made of light wood. My brother was being particularly annoying to me, so I picked one up and hit him on the head. Unfortunately for him it was one of the real ones.

Once he came around he went running off to tell mum about how I had knocked him unconscious. Unfortunately, she didn't believe him so told him off for telling tales, probably gave him a clip behind the ear. Poor brother. I think I may have had a particularly angelic face. Hope that evens things up a little.

But.... may I mention that he did get his revenge when on one year when we were having a very friendly autumnal leaf fight, he directed me to pick a lovely pile of leaves up to throw in the air. "Grab those Kate" he shouted. Unfortunately for me they were stinging nettles. I think we gave up the tit for tat after that.

Moving back to that extremely hot summer in 1976 when nana passed away. I don't think me, and my bother went to the funeral. I remember sitting on the back step of the bungalow with him for ages not saying anything. The heat was immense. Obviously, the grownups went to the funeral. Mum was all about sheltering us from death I think.

Soon after that grandpa moved down to Birmingham and stayed with us. Sometimes he would go up to Leeds to stay with mums' brother. He seemed to like the company of everyone. I can remember walking back from school and seeing grandpa sitting in the front window and the feeling of being so glad to see him. I loved my grandparents.

Mum and Dad found a flat for him in Bearwood, just down the road from where we lived. We all excitedly set it all up for him and I was really chuffed as I would be able to visit him regularly. I was a little worried as it was a first floor flat and it had had quite steep staircase for him to climb. I needn't have worried though, as he never was to move into the flat as he got poorly so continued to stay at our house at Devon Road.

It must have been strange for him, as it had once been his house and I'm sure that house must have held lots of memories for him. I unfortunately didn't help matters much because after one of my oily eczema baths (I will talk about my skin issues shortly), and me forgetting to clean the oil out of the bath as I was scatty, grandpa had a slip hitting his head on the taps.

I was in bed at the time, but I could hear him calling out for my mum. I shouted downstairs in absolute fear and mum rushed up to help him. Very quickly he was in an ambulance and he was whisked off to hospital. I felt so guilty and hid in my bedroom for hours. I didn't get into trouble as such as all the attention was on grandpa, but I remember the looks I got off my mum and I felt it was totally my fault for grandpa's accident.

Over the next few days he stayed in hospital and the church members all rallied round my mum and dropped off gifts for his return home. When grandpa was due home, mum and dad went to collect him. I was left in the house with the chocolates, cakes and other gifts. I eyed up the chocolate orange and thought no one would notice if I had a piece. Or a second piece.

By that time, I had eaten the lot and noticed I was hiding in the broom cupboard even though there was no one in the house, it was all too late. I filled the inside of the wrapper with kitchen roll and tried to make the box look as if no one had actually touched it.

When they came home, grandpa had a huge patch over his eye and he gave me a big kiss and hug (I expect he guessed how I may be feeling) I had actually forgotten about the chocolate orange as I was so glad he was home and in good spirits, until Mum picked it up to offer him some. Obviously, she found it was empty. She asked me if I had eaten it and out of fear and guilt I said no.

She asked me again and I said no. She then told me to go upstairs to think about it, and she wouldn't tell me off if I told the truth. After half an hour I thought I should come clean and tell the truth. I got absolutely screamed at. I expect that it was mum's frustration about me putting everyone in the situation in the first place but it all came out in one big shout of "GET TO YOUR ROOM!" I knew better than to argue so retreated.

Apart from that grandpa did seem to recover for a while and things plodded on. We all thought he would be ready to go into his new flat at this point but unfortunately his recovery was short lived. As he got more and more bedbound I used to hear him call out for my mum in the night and she would go in to settle him down.

I would hide under my covers. His voice was full of pain and fear. Mum would pop in to mine after and kiss and cuddle me to settle me down, but also for comfort for herself I expect.

His doctor used to pop round regularly, he was Scottish and would laugh and joke with my grandpa.

They were good friends and used to play golf together as younger men. The doctor would bring him alcohol and sit and chat with him. I presume this was because there was no chance of any recovery. It did seem odd to me that they would drink alcohol together. My grandpa was not a big drinker from what I remember.

He died in the room next to me at Devon Road. I had been sent to my friends for the night. I walked up the road the next morning to go to school past our house and mum ran out with a mars bar for me to take to school. She hugged me and sent me on my way.

On my return, I walked through the front door to see what looked like a polystyrene coffin in the hallway, the house was buzzing with people. The minister was there and as always in such situations, I was spoken to and updated with love on the situation and whisked off up to my room with a snack and a hot chocolate.

As my lovely grandpa had died in the room next to me, for some reason I had nightmares about this for years, hearing him call out. He wasn't a scary person at all, but I think it was the loss and the pain I heard in his voice in his last few weeks. I had an amazing imagination as a kid so ghosts were easy for me to imagine.

3 A Few Little Things About Me as a Child.

"I will if you won't let me", that's what I used to say when I was told not to do something. Mum used to say "you're just like the little girl with the little curl right in the middle of your forehead, when you are good you are very very good but when you are bad you are horrid!".

I don't really remember being hard work, I may have been a little pedantic and awkward. I've always had a smart mouth on me. I have always also liked to play the clown, sometimes inappropriately. I think being able to make people laugh is one of my best personality traits. I was a little smiling joker. I'm not much different now.

My brother was a bit of a star for my parents, they had high hopes that he would be a doctor or lawyer. It seemed to be the done thing for middle class parents to push the boys first back then.

We have talked about this a lot over more recent years and now that we have our own children, how they take after us in quite a few ways I really think elements of nature and nurture come into the way children progress. But it seemed dad wanted my brother to be passing exams all the time and this unfortunately just wasn't for my brother at all. He just didn't want to do it.

My cousins had all been to Oxford and Cambridge, so I think dads' hopes were that one of his children would do the same. My brother was it. I know for sure he had a lot of pressure from them, I probably escaped that. He was academic though and they were very proud of that.

For me, in fairness my skills of manipulation were far more a tune, so I could quite easily get my way. In one instance that I didn't (and I may still have issues to deal with on this matter) was family trips. My brother used to get car sick. So, did I but I used to throw up and move on. My brother made a complete drama. Sorry Bro ha ha.

I'm talking about the days of no seat belts in the back of the car, my brother got the whole back seat to recline on like some sort of ancient roman god. I got the part in between the front seats and the back seat... the foot well. Dad had thoughtfully made a shelf for me to lie on and they put a blanket and pillow to make it more comfy.

The most I had to look forward on a journey was my brother being sick on me, my brother falling on me or getting sick myself because I couldn't actually see where we were going.

To annoy the family due to my position, I would poke my head up between my parent's chairs and say "are we there yet? "at very regular intervals. In the end my brother got promoted to the front seat, dad sat in the back seat and played car games with me, and mum drove.

Mum loved to drive and also used to say she was car sick if she wasn't driving. I often think if we all were together now, we would all be taking our own cars on trips. I'm actually always suspicious of car sick people these days due to this whole car fiasco as a child.

My dad played the piano, sang in choirs and composed music so we were all encouraged to be musical. Me and my brother played the piano and he also played the guitar and me the clarinet. I think we both had a crack at the violin too. Maybe wasn't too successful.

We performed in musicals and various musical events dad organised at church. We all sang, and mum sang soprano, in an almost competitive very loud style which used to cause a mixture of laughter and embarrassment for me and my brother.

I danced, swam, as well as my music and I did these things from the age of 4. Dancing was my passion. Ballet, tap and acrobatics. Saturday mornings and one or two evenings in the week.

I performed in shows, took exams and always wanted to be best in class. I did excel at tap and ballet, always achieving good grades. I used to love achieving in this area, I felt free and just really good at it

I used to be very good at listening to a piece of music then be able to play it on the piano. My piano teacher at the time, apparently still tells the story of how I played beautifully, and when I finished playing and proudly turned around asking how I did, he pointed out my music book was upside down and on the wrong page.

I could read music, but my brain used to sort of duplicate the sound before my eyes had read it. I did sadly stop playing the piano when my sons were little. I am ashamed to say I sold my father's beautiful piano to pay for a week's food. I've never played since. Maybe I will one day, who knows?

We were part of the church youth club where we had many happy years, and we were also part of the boy's brigade for my brother and brownies and guides for me. I used to go on guide camp which was really good fun.

My daughter was also in brownies and also loved her brownie camp. These organisation's have been brilliant and I would love to have the time to support such organisation's in the future. Great things for girls and boys to do. I was never frightened about being away from home.

I loved to sell things as a kid. I would set up shop in my bedroom and my mum would dutifully come and buy the items, she had at some point bought me back.

Once a year at church we would have a charity drive, from memory it was called "sunny smiles". You would get a book with lots of smiling faces and sell each page for as much as you could, and hopefully after a few weeks have an empty book and a bag of money to give back to charity.

I particularly liked this as I felt it may be helping children like me, who perhaps weren't as lucky to have been adopted into such loving families. I was so competitive with this, wanting to get as much money as I could for this charity.

I also used to help deliver directories for friends of my mum from time to time, just to help out I liked to be involved with people.

4 Home

My home at Devon road felt safe to me. Obviously by the time I was seventeen I wanted to be always 'out there' wherever that was. But I always enjoyed coming home.

The house itself had good sized bedrooms, a large bathroom with separate toilet. A big hallway and staircase with a nice sized dining room at the front, and a living room at the back with French windows onto a patio with multi-colour paving stones, which were great for hop scotch.

The kitchen was big and square with an old table in the middle with two draws full to the brim with pencils and pens, rubbers and pencil sharpeners and various other bits and bobs which didn't have a home.

There was a pantry at the side of the kitchen with all mums cooking ingredients and equipment in. Also shelves with tin containers full of homemade cakes, jars of homemade jams and chutneys.

The kitchen led out to the veranda where there was an outside loo, for just in case situations. My rabbit used to live on the veranda in a hutch dad had fashioned from an old cupboard. There was a door which led out to the garden and another big wooden door which led out to a shared alleyway with our neighbours.

Our neighbour used to let herself in round the back and shout "Cooey" to announce her arrival, usually to advise she had paid for the milkman or something like that. It usually ended up with mum saying something like "oh Let me pay you back", then the neighbour would respond with "oh no I won't take the money", and it was a back and forth game which could go on for ages.

It was performed quite regularly. They could even get into chasing each other and trying to get the money into the others house coats. If one won, the other would post the money back through the front door when the other one wasn't looking. I used to be fascinated by this behaviour.

I could watch them for ages, I would love to sneak up on them in the garden to try and hear who they were talking about when they chatted over the fence. Ah those were the days. I just wouldn't have time for such interactions these days. I'm usually in such a hurry in life.

My Mum was a great homemaker and was an amazing cook. Her cakes and desserts were incredible, and her Cornish pasties were always a favourite with me and my brother. Right up to the last year of my mum's life, she made a real effort at Christmas. She would decorate the house.

Two Christmas trees, one in the hallway and one in the lounge, sometimes one in the front room too. I would look at the old decorations on the trees for hours. Some were from the times when candles were put on trees.

There were no candles anymore, but the holders were intricate so would still go up. In the 1980s Christmas trees were quite often made of tinsel, can you imagine how fast they would have caught on fire if we had put the candles on? Mum would be baking for weeks before Christmas the cakes and chutneys in preparation. She would suddenly become very secret, hiding objects around the house so we would all get a lovely surprise.

We would always go to church on Christmas day and come home to the smell of turkey. We never got spoilt as far as presents were concerned, but it was the effort that went into creating the Christmas atmosphere that I remember the most.

For the rest of the year, we were fortunate to have enough money for good food, nice clothes, never designer as that wasn't something we really aspired to, and plenty of day trips.

Even as an older teenager I can remember coming home a little drunk and raiding the pantry of nice cheese and biscuits and homemade cakes. It's funny how when you're there you just take it all for granted, but what I would give to spend a day at that house with my mum and dad again today... I was very lucky.

5 Health

It was apparent after a few weeks of bringing me home from the national children's home that my parents noticed I had eczema. Apparently, it started in the folds of my arms but soon covered me. As a family we then had to endure many years of care. Oily baths, coal tar bandages, steroid creams. Lots of antihistamine medicine that made me sleepy. Trips to the children's hospital etc.

On top of the crocodile skin (which is what mum used to call it) I had asthma and various allergies. I had to keep well away from animals which made me sad. One time I remember going to my friend's house and picking up her guinea pigs and cuddling them. By the time I got home my face had completely swollen up, I had such swollen eyes I could barely see.

Unfortunately, we had a family dinner with one of my grandfather's clients at a local Italian restaurant which we couldn't get out of, so I went looking very uncomfortable and slightly mortified with my face swollen beyond recognition.

Fortunately, all the work my parents put in and the care they taught me to take with my skin was so beneficial. I now, although I am still on the sensitive side have good virtually wrinkle free skin. Not bad in my late 40s, thanks to those wonderful parents. Oh, and not forgetting a very beautiful biological mother.

What's funny that in later life, when adopted dad had Parkinson's disease and it started to affect him. He told me that they were quite disappointed when they brought me back from the children's home and realised I had a skin issue, he said they had asked for a child with no health issues.

After a few weeks my skin started to turn sore and itchy which they weren't ready for. I told him perhaps he should have asked for a refund.

My skin massively improved when I was a teenager. I remember it mainly just being round my neck which was sore, and I used to cover it up with my school shirt, but eventually it just went. However, it came back with vengeance just after I had my second son. I think it could have been down to hormones. I absolutely got covered in it.

I had been getting gradually more and itchier and within a few weeks I was covered just like I used to get in my childhood. Crocodile skin all over again. I couldn't sleep, the doctor wanted to put me in hospital, but I had a 3-month-old baby so couldn't go.

I had a nurse come out to bandage me daily. It went again for a few months, but I had another breakout when my sons were a little older. It did eventually go again about a year later and touch wood I have been ok since.

My eczema did not work with the clothing materials of the 1970s. Because me skin was so bad, my clothes would stick to me during the night-time. My skin was mainly open sores, and nylon clothing would mean my mum used to have to literally peel the pajamas off me in the morning.

My nana made me little cotton mittens which I had to wear at night to stop me scratching. I remember having an infection once, I had time off school and I think it was quite bad as I remember visits from the nurse and doctor, but I remember being quite in a dream with a high temperature. I feel for anyone who suffers from such a condition. I suffered it, but it effected the whole family.

I was lucky my parents were so caring. Sometimes I would have to be off school and mum would take me to work. I would lie on the sofa in the staff room.

The school mum worked at was a big old Victorian house which had been made into a private catholic school. My dad also worked there years later.

The school cook would bring me soup and try to keep me cheery. To be fair I was always a happy and polite child, even if I looked so sore.

My determination was to prove people wrong and even though I had terribly sore skin, I still worked hard at my ballet and music. I wasn't going to let my health get me down.

As quite often goes with eczema, asthma, which I still have on and off. I used to notice this more as a teenager and used to use various inhalers and steroid tablets. I still have this on and off, but it is mainly under control. I do find that at times when it gets bad, aloe juice seems to help, I'm not sure why.

I'm not sure why. It seems mine is irritation to some forms of pollen. Tree pollen seems worse. But still do and have always excessed through it and manage it well.

Migraines started when I was in my 4th year at senior school. I remember it clearly. I was sitting in my morning history lesson when I realised I couldn't see half of the teacher. I took off my glasses and cleaned them and put them back on, but my vision was getting worse.

The sheer feeling of panic and confusion was huge. I sat feeling polite as I was shy and didn't want to make a fuss. Eventually I had to put my hand up as I felt I was going to faint or be sick. The History teacher sent me to the sick bay where the nurse called my mum.

I waited for some time with a bucket being sick and was incredibly relieved to see mum. By the time I got home the vision had cleared but I had a pain over my left eye and was sensitive to light.

Mum made a soluble pain killer and put me to bed. I remember it took 12 hours to recover and I was still left with shooting pains in my head if I moved fast or bent down for about a week later.

I have had migraines ever since. I know I must be careful not to eat cheese, wine and chocolate on the same day. I know close to my period I may get one. I know if I am run down I may get one.

I have learned to live with them. I carry the much-improved medicine which is on the market these days and take one at the first sign of the aura.

As my job involves a lot of driving, there have been times where I have had to pull over and wait for the vision to settle. Sometimes in meetings I have to quickly pop a tablet to avoid a full-on attack. Most recently I had 2 training courses in one day and suffered a double attack.

My speech and brain were a little slower. I'm sure many suffer with this. I had one in a meeting where I lost my speech and I had to go to hospital as my customers thought I had a stroke. Fortunately, I hadn't but it can be a bit scary.

I'm not sure what the best course of action for migraines is and although I battle through, I know how debilitating they are for me, but I find if I try to manage my stress levels and health it can be beneficial.

6 School Days and Religion

I know some people say the best days are your school days, that wasn't really for me. I struggled to keep up. I had terrible eczema during my primary school days which would flair up, especially in the early years.

Part of the treatment as explained in my earlier chapter was a medicine called Phenergan. I think it was a sort of hydrocortisone to stop the itching, but it did cause a lot of drowsiness, so concentration was not always good.

I also was incredibly bored. I bet there are loads of people who would have the same school memory. My daughter loves math's, I just couldn't understand it. To be fair sometimes I just couldn't see the numbers.

A few years in I was given a huge pair of NHS specs which helped, but sometimes I still couldn't make sense of the numbers.

Some days anything that was written on a board I couldn't make sense of. Anything to do with numbers needed to be drawn into pictures like parts of a cake or apple before I could even start to make sense. Mild dyslexia was noted when I was at college, only 10 years ago.

Then it was seen that I wasn't very academic. My parents tried to encourage me to do better in my lessons by helping me at home, and I know it must have been as frustrating to them as it was to me.

They were teachers and in basic arithmetic and spelling, I was seen as unteachable. I would inevitably end up in the lowest groups at school with the kids that just wanted to mess around or kids like me who were struggling.

I was really ok at anything that involved stories. So, subjects like history, religious education, English literature were ones I enjoyed. Also, music if it was practical. Although outside school I was doing dance, I wasn't very sporty. I work out a lot now, but I was not one for games. I played the usual netball, rounder's and hockey but it wasn't my thing.

I had plenty of friends and never had much problems with people. I wasn't the most popular and I wasn't the least popular kid. I was quite nervous and didn't like confrontation. I never really heard confrontation at home as curiously my parents never ever argued they co-existed, so when I did come across any confrontation, I really didn't know how to handle it.

I still keep in touch with lots of my school friends. I have recently rekindled my friendships with a few due to the wonders of social media. I fondly remember school discos and the youth club in my senior school.

In my primary school I remember our leavers show when I was Joni Michelle playing a guitar to "Big Yellow Taxi" and some of the boys were dressed as my backing singers behind me in wigs and dresses.

In senior school my memories are few, although I remember fancying a boy who didn't fancy me back. That poor guy, I think I jumped out on him at every opportunity, probably a bit of a stalker. First big crush other than Starsky out of 1970s Starsky and Hutch.

We went to church on a Sunday morning, youth club on a Sunday night and Monday night, and guides on a Friday. I never thought I was a great Christian. I always thought I was playing along a bit. Trying so hard to be good.

I used to sit in church during prayers looking around wondering what the congregation were hearing that I wasn't. They all had their prayer books and seemed to be so transfixed on something, was something talking to them? Nothing was talking to me.

One time I was sitting in my room and praying so hard to try and hear something I thought my head may explode. It was early evening in the Autumn and I was sat in the dark I saw a light shining through my window which was actually most likely my dad putting the light on in the veranda, however I decided it was a sign.

I ran downstairs to tell my parents I had been praying and heard a voice. They told me not to be so silly and people get locked up in hospitals for thinking they hear voices.

So, this was weird to me because I couldn't understand what I was supposed to be feeling then. I was good at my religious studies as the bible was full of stories which I loved, but I didn't really understand the faith bit. I felt constantly guilty about this. I'm not the sort of person that just believes without question. I still have and have always had, a curious mind.

Dad told me many years later that he actually didn't believe in it all but really enjoyed the social aspect of church and felt inwardly spiritual when he heard hymns.

He did love the stories of Jesus and always thought we could learn lessons from them as human beings. I think mum did believe the words of the bible though, although I'm sure as with everyone she had her own interpretation.

As I've got older I do think I understand both their ideas on religion, however I have my own beliefs and dad's idea of our inner spirit. I feel this when I go into cathedrals and hear evening song and choirs, but also when I reach out for inner strength.

Is this god or us? I still don't know. I just know I'm more spiritual now than ever and practice gratitude more than I ever have in my life.

7 Gorran Haven

I dreamt about Gorran Haven last night. I do quite regularly dream about this place. I think it's because it was one of the strongest memories of places I relate my parents with. It was the one time they relaxed from their busy schedules of teaching and church activities.

I can walk around that house in my mind. It was a beach cottage which sat on the front of the village as close to the beach and sea as you could possibly get.

It was a little tatty and old. I know they modernised it now as I recently found it on the internet and it looks different but recognisable, but when we were there it had a smell of oldness and slight sea salty dampness.

You literally stepped off the road into the house. It had white washed thick granite walls. The front door opened directly into the hallway which had a door at the end which was always locked. As a kid this was fascinating, but I guess it was probably just a store room full of cleaning items for when each guest left.

The hall lead into a living room which had old furnishings and a staircase hidden behind an old musty curtain up to the bedrooms. Behind the living room was a long galley kitchen, and behind that was a dining room.

The dining room had a large window with a ledge so big I could sit on. I used to love, especially on a very stormy evening, to look out to the rocky cove, the little harbor with boats bobbing around over the sea to the rocks (Gwineas Rocks) in the bay. I remember there being a buoy which flashed out there.

Anyone who knows Cornwall well knows its wild beauty and this was enhanced but my dad's stories of his childhood in Cornwall and the ghosts of his relatives. I will talk about that later.

Upstairs there was a little bathroom, a fairly dark double room facing the street and a middle room with 3 single beds. The best bedroom was at the front. You could lie in bed hearing the tide rolling back and forth or sit on the ledge and dream of pirates and adventure. Well that's what I did.

We used to go on holiday with family friends, also teachers. They had a daughter my age and quite often my brother would bring a friend to give him a boy to adventure with too. We would read books, I loved Asterix comic books which they had a collection of in the cottage and Rebecca by Daphne Du Maurier which was appropriate for the area.

We would also go to the local beach shop and buy Stephen King, Jilly Cooper and Jackie Collins, which were our holiday favorites. You could also buy chips, ice cream and snacks from the shop, so it was certainly worth a visit. There were cliffs with lovely walks to other beaches at either side of the village, which we would take regular walks across to stretch our legs.

I used to love to adventure with my brother. It was the best. He had grown with as much of a yearning for adventure as I did. We used to be sent on missions together. One particular time whilst our parents were fast asleep sunbathing, we went rock climbing, this was something we really enjoyed.

We found a small secluded beach and went looking for treasure. After some time and being unable to find any, we realised the sea was coming in very fast, and before long we were up to our knees with water and a cliff face to climb.

My brother went first, and I tried to scrabble up behind him but couldn't get a grip. The sea was getting choppier and deeper. The strange thing I remember is not feeling any fear. My big brother reached down and grabbed my little hand, pulling me up to safety. I knew I was safe with him. We were experienced adventurers.

Sometimes we would take the dingy out. The currents

were very strong, and we drifted out. We were both very strong swimmers and could see the danger of being swept out to sea. I had lost many blow-up balls in such a way and stood on the beach feeling absolutely hopeless as I watched it disappear into the distance.

Funny to think now but we waved for help and actually got a wave back from mum and dad who either didn't realise the danger we were in or were too chilled out to help.

Anyway, me and my brother decided to jump out, roll onto our backs holding onto the ropes on the dingy and paddle our feet until we reached safety. The strong current was constantly trying to temp my feet into a vertical position, so the sea could gobble me up, but I resisted, and we made our way to safety.

Can you imagine us letting kids to that these days? My brother and I had no fear. Or if we did we bit our lips and got on with it. With mum and dad being off or the entire six weeks holiday, we spent so much time away.

We were quite knowing of the dangers, the strong currents and the fast pace at which the sea could come in and swallow you up.

There was a white house up the road on the rocks where you could order freshly made Cornish pasties. The lady in the house would make them and when the flag went up the pasties were ready. We could see the flag from our place on the beach and would be sent up to collect them by running up the road which was a huge slope and get pasties for the whole family and guests. Bringing them back and sharing them out all steaming and tasty.

They were wrapped in greaseproof paper and steaming hot. I can just taste them now. I bet that lady is long gone now, but I still like to think of her creating such joy and noises of contentment with her homemade pasties

Sometimes our guests would also include Cornish cousins who would visit for the day. My dad's brother and wife and various other visitors who would make their way down to see us.

We would have trips out too. There was stock car racing in St Austell and we had a trip to the Wheal Martyn Museum Clay Works where it was believed that some of our ancestors worked.

We loved an evening visit to Mevagissey where we could all have a root around the big antiques shop or take a walk through the streets of Polperro. On most days though we had a lazy time between the beach and house just reading and resting.

One year I'm not sure exactly which year, my brother came late. He was with his then girlfriend and another mate. They decided that they would camp nearby. They asked if I wanted a walk across the cliffs with them, it was a usual walk for us across the cliffs to the next bay.

The cliffs were bathed in sun and us all hot from the walking. Chapel Point I think it was called. We set up their little tent and all sat inside. I remember so clearly us listening to Kate Bush Violin on their tape recorder.

My brother and his girlfriend took out a joint and started smoking it offering it around, I had some and loved it. This was the start of many lost years for me. I will talk about my smoking later and I know many who have smoked Cannabis all their lives and wouldn't want to give it up, but I know it stifled my creativity.

I feel I'm always playing catch up because of such wasted time. It wasn't my brother's fault. I would have found it anyway, but it's a shame it suited me so well. However, on that day it was perfect. Nothing needed doing and the sea, craggy cliffs and company was excellent.

8 Other Holidays

One holiday we went on had been recommended by a neighbour. Apparently, they had a relative who had a caravan we could use in Cardigan Bay in Wales. Mum and dad decided it would be a great chance to get in a cheap break so off we went...the usual car seating arrangements applied.

When we got there, we found to my mums' horror that it was the teeniest caravan which had been put on brick stilts and was decidedly wobbly. Carry on camping comes to mind. It was actually awful, and I can imagine my reaction now to it but in true girl guide style (mum had been a guide too) we made the best of it.

We had been advised to avoid the geese as they were a little aggressive. My brother and I started to explore. As city kids a farm was full of interest. We kept watch for the geese and went through barns, fields looking at farm sights and smells had a fantastic time.

Unfortunately, things did go sour when the geese found us. Now I'm imagining I was about 6 and my brother about 8. We ran, they chased. We got back to the caravan, my brother jumped in, grabbed my hand and pulled me in.

Unfortunately, I had grabbed onto the kitchen rail on the door and the door swung open. As I was so small, and the caravan was so high on the bricks I was suspended gripping onto the door. Mum must have been asleep because I hung there in fear as the geese came at me like I was prey., shouting help (my brother by now had retreated to the back of the caravan in shock) my mum appeared to rescue me.

Another silly holiday was when we took grandpa to Blackpool after nana died. The guest house was terrible. I found used men's blue nylon pajamas in my bed and we had a toaster that shot the toast through the kitchen hatch onto the dining room table. Which I guess in some ways was quite convenient.

Another memorable holiday was in St Davids in Wales where we rented a holiday in the middle of nowhere, but it was surrounded by fields we could run around in and if we walked for about twenty minutes we would get to Whitesands Bay and have an amazing time in the waves.

We had gone there with the same friends we went to Gorran Haven with and so there was always something going on. We were particularly in to Whoopee cushions at that time, and one of the first jokes me and my friend played was on my brother and my friends mum.

We placed a whoopee Cushion under one of the seats and my friends mum went in the room to read but didn't sit on the seat, my brother then went in and sat on the seat. The cushion worked a treat and we giggled away. My friends Mum later said that she didn't react because she thought my brother must have had an awful tummy bug and didn't want to embarrass him. My brother played along perfectly by looking slightly ill.

Again, they had lots of books, they had lots of Tin Tin comic books which I loved.

There was a road that ran past the house and us kids would sit on the gate with our water pistols squirting cars with water as they passed, I've got to be honest I'm not sure I would have been very happy if my kids had done this as it was rather dangerous for all involved. I'm not sure the parents wanted to be too bothered by it all really as they just wanted to chill out and not be disturbed by too much noise.

I remember getting told off for saying I was bored one afternoon, my mum told me not to be so ungrateful. She was right.

One year we went to Brittney, It was an adventure and the first time abroad for me. We went with my dad's brother and his wife. We went down to Plymouth where they lived and stayed there overnight before catching the ferry the next day.

We took the cars and drove off when we got to Roscoff. We carried on to a small town where we stopped over for the night in a small hotel.

I was in love straight away with the place in the morning when my mum opened the shutters of the room and we looked down onto the winding street below. We had fresh Croissants for breakfast and got on our way.

Our destination was La Foret-Fousenant where we had a large caravan for two weeks. It was a beautiful place. There was a restaurant on site where you could take your pots and pans from the caravan and they would fill it with food. I was surprised as a child as I was a fussy eater, but I loved everything I ate there.

As dad and his brother and my mum were teachers, they liked to practice French everywhere. It was embarrassing as a kid. Dad was very much into his pronunciation and used to ty and get everything right, which is admirable, but I would just tell him he was spitting. He was the same in Wales. Poor dad he was teaching us the right way to do things.

However, one day we went over to Quimper for a festival they were having and we took both the cars. My uncle stopped to ask directions from a policeman, in French obviously, thanked him then proceeded to drive off on the wrong side of the road, my dad then followed him whilst all mayhem broke out around us with cars beeping and the police men throwing their arms up in the air.

Again, as I was in my early teens, I hid down into my seat and wished I could disappear.

It was really odd also because we parked in front of a lady's house. She came rushing out to talk to us. I would usually run away at the point of a stranger running out to us, but my dad and his brother were talking away in some form of French with her and decided that she was some sort of distant relative as she had a similar name to our Cornish name.

We were all then taken inside to see her furniture. This was really strange to me and my brother. I couldn't really understand what was going on however I will always remember the Brittany Style heavy wood furniture in that house. Brittany was once a Celtic nation and the ornate hand carved furniture was inspired from Breton songs. I guess that was the Cornish link

We also visited Concarneau which had a wonderful fortified old stone town called the Ville Close. We had a lovely day there and sat on the beach where I had the biggest choux bun I could find and felt sick for the rest of the day.

I had other wonderful holidays with my parents in the UK and abroad, Crete was a lovely holiday and I was treated to my dad practicing his Greek at every available moment and mum pretending she wasn't into the ouzo but knocking it back with gusto then Greek dancing at every opportunity.

I could talk about my family holidays all day, maybe I should revisit the places for a holiday review book? I have to feel grateful for their Title for next book I think.

9 The Holiday That Went Wrong

When I was 16 I went to Lindos in Rhodes with my parents and their friends and daughter. If I'm honest we had a lovely holiday on the whole, but something happened to me that changed my life forever. I was quite the little goth at this time. Spikey hair, big hippy skirts and flowing tops and a generally "I'm too cool for school" demeanor.

My parents gave me and our friend's daughter quite a long lead as we were both quite sensible. Then one evening we went up to the local bar, it was a bar up the other side of the village by the little road down to the beach.

My friend was talking to a boy and I sat at the bar wishing I was back at the villa. I sat drinking a cocktail and smoking a roll up. Now that sounds bad for a 16-year-old I know, but even back then I wasn't the sort of teenager to overdo anything. I would have the odd drink but never liked the feeling of being drunk. With all my ailments feeling drunk didn't help.

I noticed my friend had gone so asked the bar man where she had gone, and he advised me she had gone down to the beach. So off I went after her. Unfortunately, this was a clearly a set up and I was followed by a man.

This man I had seen in the bar and had told him I was with my friend, in the nicest possible way I had told him to go away. I felt danger straight away as soon as I saw him but trying to be polite had a brief conversation with him telling him I was looking for my friend, within what seemed like a blink of an eye he overpowered me.

The whole thing happened in a flash. It's a strange thing what goes through your mind at such times. I mean I remember trying to fight it off but then had pain in my ribs and stomach. I can remember thinking I don't know how to stop this. I will have to just go limp.

I remember him telling me he would "do you from behind so you don't get pregnant." and weirdly to this day I can remember in my subconscious thinking "how thoughtful"

I mean??? What on earth was going on in my head? My body just died, and my brain just shut off. I kind of think I was brought up too polite to fight. I didn't stand a chance.

I was so annoyed with myself that I fell for the whole thing. Why had I not just waited? But I guess I was worried for my friend and that she may be in trouble. Fortunately, she wasn't.

After he had done what he had done, he wandered off. I ran, first to people I saw on the beach but there seemed to be some sort of sex party going on which freaked me out more, a woman I had seen with a man earlier on in the day who now seemed to be with lots of men and she and they were all laughing like banshees.

So, I ran off without asking any of them for help back to the square where I found my friend, perfectly ok. I told her we had to go home now and ran through the streets in a panic with her trailing behind me asking what had happened to me. I found my way to the lagoon close (St Paul's Bay) to our villa and plunged myself up to my waste in water. I stood looking at the reflection of the moon and acropolis for some time thinking why such a thing happened in such a magical place. Why????

Eventually I got out and wandered in a daze back to our villa. On the walk back, my friend and I decided it may be best not to mention this to our parents. They wouldn't understand, and they would blame us. So that was it, nothing was mentioned. Well kind of.

That night I had a strange dream. The wind was picking up outside our room and one of the shutters blew open. I looked out the window at the debris blowing down the dusty road and again up to the moon and the acropolis and felt that my life had changed.

I had bruising over my mid-section and was distant and hidden under clothing for the rest of the holiday. I never left my mother's side, but never told her. Being a bit gothic at that time came in useful, as no one really noticed if I was being a bit off or covered up in dark clothing. I continued the holiday and I put what happened to the back of my head. It was probably my fault anyway.

On my return home life went on as normal. I stayed around the home a lot more, I told my brother and his girlfriend what had happened. They told me to tell our parents, I told them no. I tried to carry on like normal, but I didn't feel normal.

I started seeing a boyfriend but always felt a sense of guilt about what happened to me. In those days it was fine for men to sleep around, but it was seen as slutty for women to do the same and although I hadn't consented to having sex with the guy in Rhodes I did feel I must have done something to ask for it.

This was extenuated by a male friend who I confided in, clearly couldn't handle the fact that it had happened to me so when under the influence of alcohol, would call me a slag and tell me that I must have really been asking for it.

Essentially, I was still dealing with the actual rape and now mental abuse and I didn't have any idea how to deal with this.

One day I made an appointment with a voluntary Rape Advisory Council. I needed to talk to someone. I poured it out to a lovely lady who also gave me some tests, I can't remember what they were for, but I'm presuming they were for pregnancy and STI's.

I also volunteered to make tea for people attending just to feel I helped. I just felt I needed to be around people who may understand. I then disappeared and didn't go back to the centre. I think often about it and felt this was the only adult help I got at that time. It meant so much to me.

However, I was clearly worried about being found out as I even gave them a false name. I felt so ashamed. I was so worried someone may know my parents and tell them, and I would have to deal with their disappointment as well as my own.

However, that move to counselling was the start of many years of on and off counselling. I still dip in now as I think sometimes it helps getting things straight in my mind.

After all these years I am returning to Rhodes for the first time. I will visit Lindos and realise I'm so over this. It wasn't my fault, there was little I could do. I was a child. I was not a slag.

Totally ridiculous nonsense we can buy into. I know that now. However, I'm sure that there will be people out there who are made to feel like it's their fault and they could have stopped it.

Why do we turn this onto ourselves as victims? Why did society make me as a victim, constantly feel I had done something wrong? What would I have done to stop this? Was it something I was wearing? Why should we not as a society have been putting the accountability of the rapist? What could he have done to stop it?

Perhaps if he had been dressed in a straight jacket he wouldn't have been able to rape someone. But no, society's way is what could the women have done to avoid being raped by a rapist. We have it totally topsy turvey. I felt at that time if I had of said anything it wouldn't have gone anyway, I would have been to blame and then to hide away with shame.

If you feel anything thing like I did I want to help you empower yourself and love yourself again. I did, it has taken a long time, and some would say I'm still learning to love myself. But I have experienced the feelings and now gone through the healing.

I made up a cover story about the rape and the lack of control and utter uselessness I had felt during it. I pretended I had defended myself and stabbed the rapist in his side, I hadn't. And to this day I'm not 100% sure why I told myself that. I think it made me feel better like I have had the last word.

I had lost control and a stranger had taken something of me away, so in my imagination I had taken something away from him. I have only recently come to terms with this untruth I told myself. I was raped, I had no control of the situation. It wasn't my fault.

As an adult I reflect through very different eyes on this rape. I have no feelings of hate anymore; however, I don't want this to happen to anyone else and would like to support those who it has happened to.

You may have read through my life so far and thought, look at you, you had a great life, you had great parents, you were lucky. I was, I agree. I want to show how a successful adoption can work and how nurture is as and perhaps has been more important in my life than nature.

However, if I can think how an improvement on the nurture side would have benefitted me, one thing stands out in my mind. I would say, relating to my parents was a problem. For all the joy, love and care they provided, I still couldn't trust them to understand what had happened to me in Rhodes.

I felt they would be disappointed in me and ashamed that it may come out in the church and with their friends. I also thought they would ground me. Now I could have been wrong and that is something I shall never know. I even gave rape crisis a false name as I was afraid my parents may find out through them. Crazy I know!

I have a daughter and I want her to be able to come to me with anything. My boys have gone through ups and downs and at times like all parents have thought "what now"? And raised my eyebrows a little. But I have supported them to find solutions and get help.

I don't feel annoyed at my parents for the way they were. They gifted me with a fantastic early start, they just didn't talk about anything to do with bodies or sex. Just was a no-go area.

Which did make it difficult when learning about relationships as a teenager as it was all seen as shameful, especially as a girl. I think times have changed. I think we talk more freely now.

It wasn't their fault though, it was the time they were brought up in, the experience they had in their families and I think perhaps it was just too uncomfortable. I'm am however eternally grateful for them finding me and loving me

10 Rockers

My brother was into rock music back in the 1980s and still is. I suppose if you put him into a box at that time, he may have been called a rocker. I being 3 years younger was greatly influenced by him.

As a 13-year-old I would see his leather jacket hanging on the chair in the kitchen smelling of patchouli oil. And think he was so cool. I would ask him if I could have some patchouli oil too, "girls have jasmine!"

He would say. "I will get you some next time I'm in town." Town to me was House of Frazer and Marks and Spencer's where I went with mum. Town Hall where I went to play with various orchestras and to watch various classical concerts with dad and the Hippodrome where I watched the ballet.

What was this patchouli smelling town my brother knew? He was also smoking. There was a gold packet of Benson and hedges cigarettes in his pocket the one day. I was in awe, but also worried he may make himself ill and get addicted, but never the less I then went on a smoking quest.

I tried to try and smoke incense sticks and me and my friend used to spend hours trying to make pretend cigarettes. My Friends dad who I see rarely still reminds me of how he could smell his cigarettes on me as I walked passed. Well come on!! Who didn't steal parents and friend's parent's cigarettes in the 1980s??

My brother eventually took me to his Birmingham. It was a lunch time in the 1980s and we walked down a tiny alley in Birmingham. It was Mr. Bills in Needless Alley in Birmingham.

It's still there but recognisable. At the doors of the pub was a guy sitting on a stool and as we descended down the stairs the smell of beer, cigarette's, patchouli and weed hit me. Loud rock music and lots of long haired people.

The tables were all wooden with wooden benches to sit on. My brothers' friends seemed to really look after me and this became the haunt of Saturday lunch times for me. Even when I got little jobs (like Mr. Wimpey and a bear in a toy shop, character building stuff which I will discuss one day when I have had sufficient therapy.)

I would still go there, hobble back full of alcohol and try to perform my job as best I could, mainly getting sacked eventually. Eventually the routine, when I had decided signing on was the best option for me, was Bills at 12.30, fast food, home for a rest, watch Robin of Sherwood then back out to the pub. Those were the days when I worried about very little. I actually felt I was healing a bit also after the awful experience in Lindos.

As well as Bills we would frequent the Costermongers, Edwards No 8, 49'ers, West End Bar (which was a bit later) and The Powerhouse on alternative night where we would plod around the dance floor to our favorite tunes of the time .

There was a girl who literally just walked backwards and forwards. Of course, this was the time before choreography, so we just used to go with the flow. I could talk a lot about the alternative nightlife of the 1980s and have lots of fond memories.

We went to concerts, one being, Hawkwind in the 1980s with my friends, It was at the Odeon in Birmingham. We arrived there late and the band had started playing. The air was so thick with the smell of weed and the music was loud and trippy.

Many years later, I took my younger son to see them in Wolverhampton when he had just started playing the guitar in his first band at school. It was considerably different from my first experience, probably as I had become a responsible parent and was driving. Ah how responsibility changes you.

Funny thing is when the band started we realised we were in the wrong room and New Order were playing. That would have been a good gig too.

I was never able to see many live bands mainly due to finances. Obviously once I had kids to support any spare money did go on them. Back in the 80s those I remember were obviously Hawkwind, The Cult, I loved Ian Astbury, and a few festival trips, Roy Harper, what was the Birmingham Polytechnic at the time, the few members of Gong playing a random gig but I can't for the life of me remember where that was.

Funnily enough it was only a few years previously that I went to watch The Nolan's, Sheena Easton and Alvin Stardust with great enthusiasm with my mum. Please erase your memory of that .....now!!! It's not cool at all.

To be fair once I became a single mum, people just stopped inviting me out with them, I lost touch with a lot of people and disappeared into my own world. I have been to see a few more bands as I've got older and my middle child is a musician who plays almost every week, so is attending festivals and actually getting paid to play. Perhaps in the future I will be able to revisit this and go to more festivals. I can hope.

When I was 17 I stopped holidaying with my Mum and Dad. After the rape I didn't much feel like going to Greece again. I would stay at home whilst they went away. I would have friends' round for the whole time they were away, and we would party and then frantically clean up the house, so it was all perfect on their return.

Most of my friends were in-between College and University at this time so we had an extra-long summer. We would walk down to the local woods and lie in the sun smoking, spend time up the pub, watch movies on video. Smoke, chill, fall out, and make up, go to parties and dance, we used to dance a lot. At the time I was very into Frank Zappa and used to dance around, joint in mouth and fall on the floor laughing with my friends. That was a great holiday.

Not long after that, things started to change for me. All my friends went to University and I was left at home. Things mainly got a bit shit after that.

11 Peace Camp

It was around 1987 when a couple of friends and I went to a peace camp in Oxfordshire. The camp had apparently been there since the 1960s and was in protest to American air bases in the UK. To be fair I didn't want us to have a nuclear war with anyone, but I also was, as always, looking for new things to experience and thought it would be quite fun.

My friend had been invited and me and another of our friends went along for the experience. Although I dressed like many of those around me and my political views mirrored those around me, looking back I was probably more indoctrinated than free thinking. I re addressed that in later years.

Once I got there I realised I could and should have probably been utilising my time better, however I was supporting a very good friend and we had a really good laugh. After being settled into a bender which seemed to have a fair amount of space we settled into camp life.

Firstly, there were no loos. Something that I was a little unaccustomed to and although I didn't mind too much doing a number wee in the bushes, but a poo was not something I was particularly happy to do. So, I did wander down to the pub from time to time with a friend to use the toilet. Leaving friend number 1 to settle in to camp life.

After a jolly old time in the pub we rolled back. On our return we stopped to talk to an old chap sitting at the top of the camp who went on to tell us that he started the camp, but it had lately got overrun by drug addicts and had completely lost its purpose. He seemed really disappointed at what the camp had become, and he seemed to keep himself at a distance to the others.

I'm not sure if he was right about the camp members, I'm sure everyone was there for their own reasons. Most of them seemed very friendly and were similar to the people I knew back home. Money seemed very important to them as with everyone else and they went on what they called "dole runs" where they drove to different places to sign on.

Not exactly sure how they did it, but it seemed they were signing on from multiple places each. Inevitably by the time they got back the money was spent. Some of them seemed to come from wealthy families too, one lady in particular liked to boast about her family's wealth but in the next sentence seemed to resent her father. She was very open about this. She seemed to be losing her hair and was generally quite agitated. I often think about her and wonder what became of her. I hope she lives well.

One morning I was awoken in my sleeping bag. This situation has stayed in my mind for its sheer unusualness. There was a man wearing yellow dungarees and was just staring at me. He looked like someone from the children's program Play School. He went on to talk about how he was the Angel Raffaele and had led the children out of Israel.

He talked about this for about 2 hours. I was stuck with only underwear on in a sleeping bag, so I wasn't going anywhere. I wasn't sure if he was going to get me to sing a song with him or murder me in my sleeping bag. But there were even stranger people than him there.

The peace camp in Oxfordshire had an almost hidden entry. The front of it grass, then a pathway up where caravans and bender tents made out of branches and tarpaulin were either side of the path. The benders were surprising large and comfortable. There was a campfire with logs around for seating. A fire pit to cook food on and a dug out pit as a toilet just out the way of everything.

There was a varying number of people there day to day. But in the time we were there people seemed to come and go. One of the caravans housed a married couple. They shouted and fought with each other. Some of the residents told us they were on Heroin. I can't confirm this either way.

There were times in the evening when a protest would take place. This to be honest I was unsure of what actually happened. They called it an action. In the pub we heard of someone breaking into the site and breaking a lamp post. Again, I can't confirm if these people did that. We did do a sit-down sing song in the road one day which was fun. We had some of the ladies from Greenham Common pass through and they seemed a lot more organised and seemed to have some sort of plan in my opinion.

I fear that the gentleman who had greeted us on our arrival to the camp was right, they had lost their way. My friend stayed there for some time. I'm sure camp life was very different after she had been there for many weeks and the countryside surrounding it was beautiful, we did a lot of walking. I think of this time quite often. I wonder what lives these people are now living. I hope they found love and peace.

It didn't take me long to realise this wasn't my thing, and me and my friend hitch hiked home and it wasn't long before I was relaxing in my garden listening to Steel Pulse on my oversized Walkman.

In retrospect I think some of residents of that camp were people who had some sorts of problems, I'm no doctor and I'm not sure if it was drug induced problems or problems caused by situations that had happened to them in life or both. I guess that's a representation of society in general.

However, I was certainly trying to get away from my problems and I was in no fit state to help anyone else with theirs at this point in time. I know there were some great people there too who had great intentions and believed in what they were doing. I think at that time lost people had become attracted to these causes.

12 Smoking

Although I wasn't a hippy, I was a big cannabis smoker.
I smoked almost at every opportunity. I mixed with
fellow smokers and spent my days thinking about
smoking. It seemed to dull my thoughts. I was and still
am busy minded and always up to something, but
because everyone else made it clear I wasn't academic
and put up restrictions for me.

I generally believed my uselessness. I mean to be fair, a
complete stranger had used me as if I was nothing, so I
felt my value was low. I even had someone tell me
"even your birth parents gave you away, you should
think about that!!" To be fair I had no intention to
think about it.

Why would I want to nurture an entrepreneurial mind
when not only did that seem to be looked upon as silly
and unachievable for most, for me being so stupid, it
was out of the question?

So I smoked. Splits, bongs, pipes, hot knives you name it I've smoked weed like it. I didn't smoke much in those early days, but after the incident in Rhodes I used it to block my feelings of inadequacy.

Sometimes I would sit at the top of my garden at home and smoke it, I was unemployed so had not much to do, or go to the woods and meet up with friends to smoke.

We watched shit TV on little black and white TVs and getting stoned. We watched the gong show and other crazy day time programmes and chilled out. It was great, I had no more expectation of life but to sit in damp bed sits and listen to people put the world to rights. As people who seemed to know so little at this time we seemed to be experts in everything.

There was always a wise expert at hand to explain the meaning of life to us all. I used to not give too many opinions because I was a girl. I was under the impression I was stupid, pretty, but stupid. I doubt my friends would say they thought I was stupid at all, but this was my perception and how I felt.

My good friends who didn't smoke as much went off to universities around the country and had fuller lives at that time. The whole smoking situation was getting really out of hand in the end and I knew it. On top of the depression, I was suffering panic attacks. I would get them all over the place, I would get hot and cold at sudden intervals, wouldn't be sure if I was going to be sick or faint.

I had terrible light sensitivity and at times would wear my sunglasses through whole movies at the cinema. At one point whilst lying in bed smoking, I literally thought I was having a stroke, my hands went all cold and positioned themselves in a claw shape and I started to pass out.

My partner called 999. It was a panic attack. Since I've stopped smoking this hasn't happened again. My depression went, and I feel confident and less paranoid.

My addiction was so bad at times I would be tearing the house apart to find any scraps of weed when I thought I was out. I would be literally crawling around on my hands and knees looking in every nook and cranny.

Again, I stress I am totally for medical cannabis and would certainly look at its potential in the future to help if needed, but something in the street version did not affect me positively after long term use. I'm sure all things effect each individual differently, so again on this subject I talk from my own experience.

I was talking to a colleague the other day about a trip she is going on to Amsterdam. It took me right back to my trip in the 1990s. I don't remember the exact year. Was rather a blur. Me and my husband took two trips.

As you can imagine, Amsterdam is a rather alluring place to go if you are a stoner. And it was an exciting experience for us.

The two years we visited we stayed in different hotels. The first hotel was almost underground with iron bars at the window, rather like a prison, the second was a boat. They were both the cheapest accommodation we could find.

Obviously we were like children in a sweetie shop. Places where you could smoke in public. It was great. We just sat and smoked then found food to fulfil our munchies. I can highly recommend the sugar apple donuts they sell in the street.

We did boat tours and various other things which, unfortunately I can't really remember. Funny. What I do remember is eating some nice cake, wandering around, needing the loo and not being able to find one.

We did find a bar, I remember it having a glass walls. Anyway no one was in there apart from a mean looking man. We asked if we could use the loo and he said yes, but made us uncomfortable.

The loo was upstairs. I must explain this all happened under complete mistrust and paranoia from our side. We went upstairs but on the way down an altercation had started between the mean guy and another mean guy who had just entered. Like some angry beef going down. That is my last memory of that day. But it seems we did other things.

When we got home we noticed a load of pictures from that day. We seemed to be all over the place. One picture was of my husband with his arm round a guy and they were both smiling. We for the life of us

---

couldn't remember who the guy was but he looked strangely familiar. It was weeks later when we found the Madam Tussauds wax works tickets and realised the mystery guy was Eddie Murphy. A whole afternoon lost but clearly a good one.

Let that be a lesson to the cake lovers. We were hardened smokers, but the cake pushed us over our limits, however it was a great holiday and a great experience.

It took me a long time to give up smoking weed. I was Thirty-four when I packed it in. It was hard as I loved to smoke. I went to see a counsellor to get support. I suffered insomnia and cramps for months, but it was worth it.

My eldest son will say he noticed a change in me. I gave up a dead-end job, went to college and my life totally changed. I often wonder how my life would have looked without contact with weed.

I think I would have achieved more but looking back is not productive. I see my life now as a world of possibilities and positivity. I'm not at all stupid!!!!

13 Mum Leaving Us

My mum was such a lovely lady. She was outgoing and friendly. Everyone loved her, and she would do anything to help people. She loved me and my brother so much. We were so lucky to have her. She would run us to clubs, look after us if we were ill, inspire us, cook us treats and make our clothes (mine more than my brothers). She was great at needlework and craft. She would make up songs, jokes and cuddle us till we couldn't breathe.

She loved to throw a party, she was, as with her singing, quite competitive with the other ladies in the church. Mum loved a holiday and would spend time playing in the water and sand with us. She would tell me about the childhood growing up in Yorkshire.

I always enjoyed her stories of her schooling and how all the girls had to line up in height order and march around the school. She was the tallest in the class so was at the back, my later to be Auntie was the smallest in her class which was the class above my mums, so she was at the front.

They became friends through familiarity of marching in a row, mum being tall and auntie being small. She said there were prefects standing at the sides of the corridor who would poke them with canes if they stepped out of line. It's funny that in the future they would become sisters in law.

She was religious and had some very old-fashioned views about sex before marriage. She used to just tell me not to do it, there was very little conversation. We didn't talk about periods either, I was just directed to a bag in the bathroom and just got on with it myself. I think this was quite common in those times. She could be very strict, but very funny too.

She kept her wing of safeness around me in her mind, but some of the things we didn't discuss I could have done with discussing with her. Perhaps I would have been better armed in life.

In her defence, she was doing her very best and perhaps those subjects had not been discussed in her family either. My only regrets were that there is so much I didn't say to her. Maybe I didn't appreciate her as much as I should have, I didn't know what was going to happen though.

She was very active, badminton club, lady's guild, choir, flowers for the church along with many other things added to the running around for me and my brother. She was quite outgoing and liked to be the centre of attention.

Mum loved sport, she would take her sun bed along with the TV out onto the patio and watch Wimbledon. She really loved tennis. One time she got caught by the police for speeding trying to get home for the finals of Wimbledon. She was most inconvenienced by the whole situation.

She used to tell me how she used to dance the jitterbug in her younger days and be swung around by Americans who came over during the war. She was quite the opposite of dad really. Sometimes I would notice that he would give her a look of "enough now". She would tell me about the importance of letting one's husband think they were in charge. I'm not sure that I carried this though in my life.

The next part is a lesson to all of us of how fast life can change. You must never take too much for granted.

A few years after the Rhode's trip something really weird happened. I found myself pregnant. Well it was a result of my action; however it did take me by surprise being young and naive.

A few months previous to this event, I had come home to find mum in my room, according to her she had been looking for something and had found a bag kept I my cupboard where I had kept my contraception tablets. She was so annoyed with me and said having sex before marriage was wrong. She basically told me to stop taking them.

As I was emotionally immature, and this was certainly a conversation I could have with my mum I did, but didn't stop having sex, hence getting pregnant. Had I been older and wiser I may have had a better counter argument.

However, my mum as I mentioned was Christian and didn't believe in sex before marriage, so the conversation was a nonstarter. So, once I found I was pregnant, I kept it very secret, I knew it would be really frowned upon in our family social circle.

One night I went to an all-night party and one of my friends' houses. I stayed up all night and walked home the next day. Bathed and sat downstairs watching an old film. My plan was to see the parents, then go to bed for a few hours.

It was about 11am and I was starting to think it was a strange thing as my mum and dad weren't around. I could hear them talking upstairs so eventually I decided to find out what was up as it would have been unusual for them to be bustling around, asking me what I had been up to etc. I entered the bedroom to a weird atmosphere. I asked what was wrong and my mum just came out with it. "Your dads having an affair!" Dad was curled up on the floor in what looked like a foetal position.

For some strange reason I decided that it was the right time to say, "I see, and I'm pregnant." Looking back, it must have been total overload for them. I didn't get told off that's for sure.

Before I knew it I had ran out of the house and down to a family friend and had a bit of an outpour of emotion. It was all a lot to take in. Dad was having an affair, I was pregnant, and things were going to change dramatically. Mum eventually found me and assured me we would be ok, and she would take care of me, but dad left us and mum was shattered.

After dad left it was just me and mum in the house. She was trying so hard to get on with it. She kept talking to me of the shame. How dad would come back. He didn't. She put her efforts into caring for me and I was a typical teenager who was more worried about myself.

I can remember one day I saw her crying. I cringe at this whole conversation when I look back. I basically told her to pull herself together, I also then (I'm cringing to even revisit this) told her that if she hadn't told me to come off the pill I wouldn't be pregnant. For the first time in my life, she slapped me, right across the face. Not hard but it shocked us both and both cried so much at that moment. Two lost women.

For the next few months I watched my tummy get bigger and my mum get weaker. She died on the Mother's Day in 1988 two weeks before I gave birth to my eldest son. The night before I went to see her in hospital. There was a room full of her church friends and her closest acquaintances.

She was unconscious. She had an ovarian cyst which was cancerous.

The Doctors had said it had multiplied at a huge rate which can apparently happen in stressful situations and of course my mum had certainly been stressed.

The operation seemed to have gone well and a few days earlier she had been in good spirits. Unfortunately, something had gone undetected and she had internal bleeding that wasn't picked up until it was too late.

I had stood by her side that evening in the hospital. I couldn't cope with staying as she didn't look like mum. It was a dreadful time. She was unconscious. My dad was there by the side of her and I remember thinking that was strange he was there as he had left her.

In my sorrow I wondered if maybe he was responsible for this? I realise he of course wasn't. On a visit to my mum a couple of days earlier, Mum had told me about a dream she had. In the dream, she was lying in her hospital bed and dad had visited her. She said she had leapt up, grabbing a jewelled sword from under the covers and with great force pushed it right though him.

I remember being quite shocked by her telling me this, and as I stood looking at her and dad I wondered if she would awake and grab her jewelled sword and kill my dad right in front of us all.

Obviously, this didn't happen. But looking back mum and dad had been married for 28 years. Dad must have felt absolutely awful and not known what to do for the best.

He must have felt slightly responsible although it was really just one of those things. I was very heavily pregnant, and it was all too much. I had to get out, I was feeling light headed and just couldn't cope with the situation. My brother was being very restrained and talking to people who had arrived to show their respects.

As I rushed to get out, I have a really odd memory of my mum's solicitor saying to me, "if your mum wakes I will get her to sign these forms so that you are looked after." I'm not sure what those forms were, but she never woke.

The next day I was at my friend's house where I was staying at the time. I saw my brother and a family friend drive up to the house. I knew then she had gone. I just stood there. I was due to give birth in two weeks and I lost the one person who would have taken care of me and my baby, although I had felt let down at times with our lack of communication.

However, I had started to feel that with my dad leaving we had the opportunity to both learn more about each other. Mum really was a fantastic mum and she would have thrived on bring a nana, but that future had gone and there was no way of getting my old life back. Things were about to change again for me.

That day, once my brother left, my friend invited a load of his mates round thinking that the company may help me. I have experienced the feeling of loneliness and isolation when with others many times, usually in marriage to be honest, but this was an extreme moment of that.

I went through the motions but was in total solitude. I can only imagine my friend was trying to make me feel better, or maybe it was his way of coping and didn't want to be left on his own with me and my grief.

I'm sure I am not the only one who has felt this, but how strange it is to see when you are in a funeral procession, locked in your grief, the world carrying on as normal outside.

I was very close to my mum and my regret for losing her so early still hurts to this day, and under such circumstance. I can remember the pain of her leaving felt not only emotional, but physical. It hurt, and it hurt bad.

Soon after she died, when sorting through the family house before the sale, we found a draw in her bedroom dressing table where she had put knitted baby clothes she had collected for me, and a letter for me and my brother saying she would probably not come home from hospital and we should go on to live our lives to the full and learn to forgive.

That day feels still in my memory, and I had no idea she was collecting clothes for my baby or that she had a feeling she wouldn't be coming home. I guess if she had of come home she would have torn up the letter and no one would have known.

I had my new born son in a Moses basket which had been handed down by one of my mum's friends and sat in the back room of the house and reflected on the times we had there.
Looking back, I know I was suffering such loss, still feeling hurt and stress from the experiences I had gone through.

Grieving for my mother who had my heart so tight. I was a new mum with a beautiful baby and an insecure relationship, worried about the future. The thought of one of my kids or anyone else's children having such compounded stress at such a young age with no one really equipped to give support, does make me want to stretch out my hand as a beacon of hope.

I remember going into my bedroom and seeing all my belongings that had at one time made me feel secure and looked after, now just look like items. This was a very sad time for me. Loss is tough, but something that visits us all.

I did not recover for a long time. I carried on as I had a small baby. He kept me going and I was resilient. I didn't stay with his dad. It just didn't work. We were both young and had suffered so much loss at an early age and couldn't seem to help each other's healing. We had to go our separate ways.

I spent a few years in shared accommodation and even for a while had to leave my son at his dad's as I didn't have anywhere to take him. I can remember I didn't cry much at all. I just existed. I stayed in a women's refuge for a little while, on friend's sofas and then met someone and tried to forge some happiness.

I had grief, shame, weed and a new baby boy. I felt what happened to me was probably expected by some. Having a baby young with nothing but the pity I saw in the friends of my mother and father.

It's funny because when I've discussed this time with some of my friend's parents who knew my mum back then, they have asked me why I didn't go for help from them. They would have kept me safe. I was too ashamed.

I was also dealing with my post trauma from the experience in Rhodes which I clearly hadn't dealt with, loss of my mother, birth of a child and a failed relationship by the age of 20.

I just felt very alone and wanted to just disappear and hide. I wondered many times how would I cope? But something inside me started to fight back, I had started to become resilient I think.

Sometimes to cope I think we do retreat, looking back I may have given myself an easier time by knocking the doors of my mum's friends but perhaps I did need to regroup and lean to cope on my own.

It's funny to think that if all these things hadn't happened, my story would have been very different.

14 Dad

Dad was from St Austell in Cornwall. His mum was a housewife and his dad was a bus driver. They lived in a council house and he had an older brother and a younger sister.

He would tell me about his childhood which was heavily revolved around The Methodist Chapel and schooling. He said they didn't see much of the Second World War in Cornwall or snow, which he saw for the first time when he moved to Birmingham.

He told me once about how he had a new pair of Suit shorts on one Sunday but decided to go home a different way and tore them on a stile. He hid for some time as he thought he would be in trouble and eventually went home and was scolded for his carelessness and made to sit on the stairs for the evening with no dinner.

This is about as naughty as dad got. Dad loved showing us around places in Cornwall where he had lived and visited as a child.

He loved Charlestown and Mevagissey which are both well worth a visit if you're in the area. Dad used to wear quite formal wear, even in the summer, he also was a Jesus sandals and socks kind of guy. I loved my dad so much.

He became a History teacher in a Grammar school in Birmingham, later to become head of history. He loved cricket and ran the cricket team and the cross-country team.

He was a great dad. He showed me how to do loads. Decorating, riding a bike, my joy of playing musical instrument. He taught me history in a very visual way which has stayed with me all through my life. He would make up stories at the drop of a hat.

He was straight laced but used to occasionally let his guard down by making quite witty rude carry on type jokes. He never swore and was generally good natured. I always knew I could get round my dad easier than my mum who was much wiser to sneaky tricks.

As my dad was the music guy at church, he followed in a long history within the church of putting on what was known as "The Men's Concert". It was a yearly event held in the church hall which had a big stage with heavy red velvet curtains.

All the men of the church joined in this concert, and sketches were set out for a full night of entertainment. There were men dressed as women, obviously and the 1970s cheeky humour all the way through.

They took it very seriously and as a child I watched this showbiz glitz with wonder. The main event for me was the UV item they did when all the lights went off and we marvelled at UV underwater scenes. The men performing this were in black clothing with UV props. It was kind of high tech for the time I guess.

This would be a sell-out event in the local area. Everyone loved it. My mum and the other ladies would be preparing refreshments and getting the makeup on to the men. It was busy back stage. I always wanted to be back stage but would get told to stay sitting at the front because I would get in the way, so I did.

One year they decided it was time to bring the ladies into the show. I think it ran for two more years then stopped. I think the men had less fun working with the ladies so pulled the plug on it. However, I think these concerts were very much a thing of their time.

Dad also used the organised shows with a yearly visit from the local care homes. I was always roped in to do a tap dance. Dad would play the piano.

I wasn't the most enthusiastic about this and quite often complained about feeling like being a performing monkey, but we were always taught to muck in on such occasions so there was no getting out of this. It felt embarrassing.

But on one occasion in the middle of my performance of Chattanooga Choo Choo a man ran up to the stage and threw two pennies at me which hit me hard in the side of the head.

Fortunately, after this I was allowed to take a back seat on this event. On reflection, I was probably giving the audience a nice afternoon by tap dancing for them I hope I did.

I had a few clues in my years at home that dad although wonderful as a dad, may have a slightly roving eye.

Firstly, he sent mum flowers when on a choir trip. They arrived at our home and mum seemed genuinely happy but also a bit confused. It wasn't her birthday and it was a little out of character. I also thought it was strange.

Also, one year when I had stopped going on holiday with mum and dad they had booked a two-week holiday in Kos. I had stayed at home and dad had stayed at home for one week, planning to join mum on the second week.

That week I had decided to dye my hair blond, unfortunately it had gone pink. Well salmon. I was in such a panic, and thought dad would be cross with me., but when I went downstairs he was in the living room entertaining a lady and they were both drinking sherry. Sherry at about 1pm which was unusual.

Anyway, he introduced me to the lady and said my hair looked nice. Weird. I knew something wasn't right. So, when the news came out, I wasn't too surprised. I know as an adult that you can just fall out of love.

It happens. I do wish my mum had of held on a bit longer as she would have come out of the depression and found a new life, with a wonderful grandson to spoil. Also, similar situations happened with some of her friends and she would have found some help and comfort with them.

Clearly after dad's affair and mums' demise, things were strained between us. I moved from place to place with my boy. Dad would turn up now and then and try and help me, financially usually. I was in shared accommodation so at times my son would have to live at his dads. I hated that so much.

When I went to see him, I was not treated so great by people I had once thought were friends. But I fought on through. I eventually found another partner and my dad gave me money to put down on a house. We bought a little 2 up 2 down in Handsworth Birmingham and I was able to have my son back. We married shortly after and had another son.

This didn't work out, so I ended up alone again with the two boys. Ok I've put not much information on that relationship. I think it's not about my son's fathers and I wouldn't really want to write about my relationships. I'm actually not great at relationships historically. I get hurt and then shut down completely. I think that could be another book entirely.

Dad and I worked hard to build up our relationship again. Eventually we became dad and daughter again and all the pain and disappointment went away.

Dad helped me bring up the boys through very tough years. I was in constant depression and smoking lots of cannabis to try and lessen the stress. I would then end up on anti-depression tablets and so on in a cycle for many years.

Through those years dad supported me. Financially and emotionally as best he could. Making sure I had food in and the boys were cared for. I loved the boys so much but found parenting and my own thoughts a challenge at times. I would quite often while away the day being stoned.

When I had an eczema flair up one summer, my dad suggested we went to a Chinese herbalist to get treatment. My eczema had been so bad I think partly to hormones after having my second son. The treatment worked with perseverance and going through something new like that with dad away from conventions brought us together.

We had to boil herbs in a big pan, separate it into drinks so I could have two drinks per day. I also had to add to the bath the herbs left in the pan and have a good soak. It was a lot of hard work but miraculously it worked. I've not been as bad since this treatment and would recommend it to anyone who has eczema and who can stomach the taste of the treatment.

I had to have a glass of squash next to me when I drank it. So sour. I also went through a spate of tonsillitis in the 1990s and dad took care of me, taking me to hospital on a Saturday evening to get antibiotics.

He would also spend time in the garden with the boys, making it beautiful. He did the same in the house I live in now. I have two rose bushes he planted that give me a beautiful gift of huge red and pink roses each year. It makes me feel that dad is still in my garden watching over me.

After staying so silent about the incident in Rhodes for years I eventually had a conversation with dad one day when we were sitting in his car. I told him that I had been attacked on one of our family holidays. I didn't go into any details, just told him when and where it happened.

He put his hand on my hand and we never mentioned it again. Did he believe me? I don't know. He may have not wanted to. I can't ask him now, so I shall never know. I do think that perhaps it was my perception all along that my parents wouldn't understand what had happened to me.

I never really gave them the chance as I was so scared of letting anyone down. I bet there are plenty of people who will run away from problems instead of reaching out to those who love them unconditionally. Interestingly though, our relationship strengthened a lot after that.

Dad went on to take me and the boys on holiday to Cornwall and the Lake District, and the boys talk to this day about the many trips they went on with their beloved grandad. He would look after the boys during the school holidays when he wasn't teaching so I could work.

My eldest son was subjected to dads teaching skills and kept in to learn sometimes when his brother ran around outside. Dad had this thing about the eldest son being successful. I don't think that is always so. We can all be successful in our own ways, I guess it's how you measure success.

As I have mentioned before, I truly believe it's not always measured in academia. There was many a time when we were out as a family and a stranger would walk up to my dad and say that they were students of his many years ago and had great memories of him. That always made us proud. I think dad touched many people's hearts, so he was truly successful in that way.

15 Being a single mum

I had my second son at my two-bedroom terrace house in Handsworth. Not too long after that my marriage failed, and I became a single mum.

I was a young single mum with two very energetic boys. I was still very lost, isolated and immature but worked hard to try and do my best. This was difficult and quite lonely for me. I had two beautiful sons but was lonely as an adult.

When they were little and before I learned to drive, I would walk with one in the baby buggy and one holding onto the buggy down to the local supermarket. Do the shopping, balance as much as I could on the buggy and walk home. If I managed this without a one of them having a complete screaming fit, that was a good trip.

They would fight and fight as boys do. They were mischievous and would regularly try my patience. The boys would go to their dads at the weekend which would give me a bit of respite.

We had animals, the first one was a cat called Precious who after a couple of years got run over. My eldest son was heartbroken but my youngest was not really that bothered. He actually stated he wasn't that fond really.

He was usually to the point. I got another kitten and she got pregnant as I hadn't had her spayed. She had about 7 kittens in front of us, which was a good experience for me and the boys. We cared for the kittens together until they were ready to go to new owners. We took our cat to the vets after and there were no more kittens.

I would walk the boys up to school and pick them back up. At 5 pm we would curl up in front of the television together and watch Star Trek the Next Generation. We all loved it and I would make tea. When I was particularly short of money, I would gather together all the left overs I could find around the kitchen and serve them as bits and bobs. It may consist of a sausage roll, noodles, bread and butter, and a cup cake.

Bits and bobs became their favourite meal. My oldest son enjoyed salads and fish and my youngest enjoyed a Sunday dinner. I always cooked lots, making the most of what I had. Mostly I had more than bits and bobs and was able to make vegetable chilli's, lasagne, salads and roasts. I also learnt West Indian cooking from my neighbours which always went down well with the boys.

We had a lovely garden at the back of the house which the boys helped their grandad tend. The gardens were joined by a pathway in between the yard and the garden. Three houses shared the alleyway and we were in the middle, so there was always coming and going at the back of the house.

I recently asked my sons about their memories of those times and these were what they came up with

- The one neighbour breaking into the other neighbour's house and stealing the contents.
- They used to hear a mobile phone constantly ringing in the wall of their bedroom.
- Being sent to the corner shop and being chased by stray dogs. There was a gang of stray dogs that used to hang around and chase everyone.
- Us adopting a crazy dog which we had to send back
- Doing the garden
- Long summer days
- Watching Star Trek
- Days out with grandad
- Holidays

There memories aren't that bad I think, although the neighbours stealing from each other was not great.

My youngest son had night terrors from really young. He could wake up shouting out or actually walk around and talk but actually be asleep.

As the two of them used to share a room quite often he would wake his older brother up by just standing by his bed in a weird sleep but eyes wide open way. And I would get a call from my older son to come and settle him down. He also used to come downstairs and talk about strange things and I would have to take him back up. I would never wake him but just calmly put him back in bed.

Once he came downstairs when I was with a friend and was rather stoned and asked if we knew where the diplomatic bag was, and he then stormed off into the broom cupboard where I retrieved him from and carefully popped him back up to bed. If anyone has witnessed sleep walking it can be really odd. I'm not sure if he still does it. I will have to ask his girlfriend.

Dad helped me so much looking after the boys. He tried to educate them, he taught them how to garden. Took them to his school in the holidays so they could help him with odd jobs. Sat and watched the TV, took them on holiday and generally tried to support me in being there for us all.

We would go to dad's school firework nights and he would parade us around introducing us to people and treat us to hot dogs and jacket potatoes. We loved his firework night. One year when the boys had been particularly naughty arguing and fighting, I had to cancel our visit. I think it was probably worse for me to do that as it was a link to the outside world and a treat for me.

Dad would work with me on the house all the time. I could always rely on him to help me with my decorating and any DIY that needed doing. He was always there to help. He didn't want to do it all for me though, he made me work with him. Which has given me some great lessons and skills.

16 Dodgy Goings on

This is the hardest part to write. You may think I've had more challenging parts but no. The other situations, adoption, rape and loss situations that were out of my control.

But this I did myself. I do think it was definitely born out of the environment I was in at the time and the way I was feeling about my self-worth and what I could do in life.

However, I feel I should have known better. I've spent a long time thinking about the best way to write this part of my story. I am going to leave some of this up to you to decide what's real or not. But I will try and discuss it as openly as possible.

When I lived in Handsworth, after my divorce and as I was bringing up my two boys, I was going through a massively confusing time. It was a really strange culture where I was living in at this time in the 1990s.

There seemed to be a confusion of right and wrong. Crime was seen as good in the area and goodness was seen as bad. Robbery, drug dealing, and violence seemed to be seen as good. Going to prison was seen as a badge of honour.

I'm not going to say I got totally sucked up into this, but I partially did. At the time I was struggling financially. It was the time when the milk man used to come and do the rounds and I was struggling to even pay him. I used to get the boys to hide with me in the living room and keep quiet until he had gone away.

Things were just getting out of control. This was not the first or last time I've been at rock bottom with finance. It's really all to do with my poor management of my own personal finance. I'm still learning to get that right and I think I am at last getting there with that. Some may say "about time too!"

With money getting very tight dad was more or less supporting me, and the Children's dads were doing their best to help and were helping their boys.

However, I hated that and I wanted to be more independent. I didn't want anyone else supporting me, but also wasn't really in the know to get the right advice. I was not very experienced in looking after a house financially, and I really think still to this day we don't teach our kids this.

To help my situation I decided to look for a job. The trouble was I had 2 boys to get care for and that was going to cost more than I could earn. Even when I did get an interview as a secretary the interviewer asked me "so you're one of those scrounging single mothers we here about on the news" my answer was "obviously not as I'm trying to get a job".

At that time the media was talking a lot about single parents, so I guess that trickled into the general public's opinion. Needless to say, I didn't get the job. Practically I would have been working for nothing anyway once the child care had been taken out of my wage. So, I gave up!

One day some bailiffs arrived at my door telling me I had not paid the poll tax. I realise now I could have got various benefits for that, but at the time no one had advised me, so I was only claiming the job seekers allowance which wasn't much. I couldn't afford to get a job as I had two kids under school age and there was nothing to help with care at that time. Later on in life I was able to claim tax credits and go back to work.

The bailiff's advised they could take 3 courses of action to pay for this bill.

1/I pay in full in 2 weeks

2/I give them something in the house which would cover the debt although they didn't feel I had anything that would cover.

3/they took me to prison for the amount of time allotted for no payment of council tax.

Clearly 3 was out of the question. I had 2 young children. 2 was doubtful, so number 1 was the only option. I had to find the money within 2 weeks. I actually seem to work well under pressure, so my brain clicked in to working out how I could make that sort of cash in 2 weeks.

Thinking on my feet, I thought of options. Getting a day to day job was not going to fix this. I would not be able to raise the money in two weeks in that manner. I realised a "working from home" job was my only option.

Packing parcels? Filling envelopes? No that wouldn't work. It's funny how ideas formulate in your brain at times like these. I remembered a friend of mine talking about a friend who ran a promotion agency and introduction escort agency outside the Birmingham area.

I decided I may be able to get some work from them. I wasn't actually thinking I would work for them but was wondering if they would let me run a sort of franchise of their business. I remembered them saying they did very little in Birmingham and I thought I could just cover this area.

I made the contact very quickly once I had made up my mind this was my best course of action, it's amazing what you can do when you're under the threat of prison for non-payment of poll tax. I arranged a meeting with them away from my home and put forward a business idea.

My idea was that I would run and grow their business in Birmingham and they would pay me fairly. Yes, very naive I know! But remember I had no experience of such things, I was literally just working from my instinct.

The business itself seemed a little confusing. They had ladies and men on their books who they would make introductions to customers. They charged a fee for the introduction and insured the safety of the employee as best as they could.

Sometimes the ladies and gents would accompany people out to events. Sometimes not. The not became more apparent as times went on. You couldn't discuss any other transactions than the initial introduction with the clients. Ok so we kind of all know where this is going don't we....

My first job was to get some people to work for my part of the franchise. This was not an issue at all I learnt this very quickly. Firstly, you put an advert in the paper Escorts required for new Birmingham Agency and you wait.

Calls started very fast. In those days I had a house brick of a phone and also had a portable phone at home. I took calls day and night and made contacts.

I had to go out to interview the potential escorts which was more difficult. How they sounded on the phone and how they were when I met them was quite often very different. I was at that moment doing all the hiring, phone calls advertising on my own so every day was a school day.

I think in my head I had the vision of sophisticated men and women working in the agency, and sometimes when I got around to visit them this was not always the case. I was also quite often propositioned by the ladies asking if they could show me their skills. It seemed that for some of these girls that was something they expected to have to do which is a shame.

I think they must have worked for some far more demanding employers than me in the past. This made me more determined to create a nice environment for them and even though I had to at times be tough as business can push you that way, I would give them as much protection as I could.

I did later on manage to get some rather good connections who I could call on if there was any issues. Fortunately, I am a cunning woman and had so far managed to smart mouth my way out of most situations that have arisen.

I eventually got a team I was happy with. About 40 ladies and a few gents. The gents didn't seem to be very much in demand, however I had plenty of calls from gents wanting to be escorts, but no calls of ladies or men wanting male escorts.

Perhaps that's changed now? I don't know as I have been out of the industry for many years. Out of the 40 only around 10 actually worked.

Most of the escorts were nurses and carers strangely enough. They would all say they were supplementing their low wages. Some said they had made more from the escorting industry than they did with their day to day careers, however they were bright enough to know that they needed to maintain a full-time career with pensions and holiday pay.

I would put a call in to the newspaper on a weekly basis to advertise the business, and the calls from customers would roll in. I had to be very careful on the phone though as I was just the connection between the escorts and the customers, I could only offer the service of an escort to accompany them to events of an introduction for their time of which I charged a fee. Once the escort was with the customer, anything they agreed to do with them was their business.

I'm going to tell you some stories they told me about their visits. These were not necessarily whilst they were working with me as I was only making introductions, but they were certainly an interesting conversation.

I'm literally only telling you about them because all these men would have been the sort of people who would generally be looking down their noses at others being in positions of authority.

They may well have also looked down on the ladies providing the service too which again seems odd. It does to some extent expose a certain type of gentleman who had gone past the norms and moved into completely different world of gratification.

There was once a man of influence who came from Manchester. He was very much into strange things. He liked to dress up as a gimp in a full latex body suit. He would have something in his mouth (which was part of this suit) which he would blow up with the use of a pump in his hand which would take him to the point of asphyxiation. At which point he would climax into a condom and drink the contents. (I do hope you're not reading this on an empty stomach I'm so sorry if you are). He would then enjoy a good spanking with a paddle until he climaxed into another condom and would again drink the contents. The girl would be asked to go into the bathroom and clean up while he would make a nice cup of tea (which she wouldn't drink after all she had witnessed) and have small talk with her before tipping her and bidding her farewell.

There was once a man who liked to plunge a whole hand inside a lady. He again was a person of great influence. He said he had seen this in magazines when he was at university and it had stayed with him ever since. He used to tip the ladies well and would tip the agency extra for the introductions. He was a very polite man.

There was once a man who had many different fetishes and an unquenchable thirst for many ladies at once. His favourite thing was to have two ladies turn up at different times, they would be expected to let themselves in the large house and follow his instructions left around on little bits of paper. One would go outside, weather permitting and be asked to undress and complete various tasks. This may be some naked lawn mowing or reading pornographic magazines or pretending to be asleep. The other would go upstairs and undress, she would then be joined by the man and together they would watch the girl in the garden complete her tasks. He would then instruct the girl to join the girl in the garden where the man would instruct the girls in how they should pleasure each other. He would eventually bring himself to climax and the girls would be told they could leave and their tips would be left on the sideboard as they exited the property.

These were some of the stories that I was told. As I love stories, these have stayed with me. Although they are gruesome. I must say that it makes you wonder about some of these people in responsible roles, how responsible are they? Why do they require this sort of hobby?

One year when the Motor Show came to Birmingham things got really busy. I was getting calls from abroad from potential customers who wanted escorts but were finding it difficult to get into hotels, so I had to end up booking their hotels for them as well as their escorts for the night. I had ladies meeting up with people all over Birmingham. It was nonstop!

I had a large booking in one of the big hotels for a dinner dance and had to send 5 escorts, however when they got there the men had also ordered escorts from other agencies too and the ladies had started fighting each other in the corridor. The men had retreated to a room to avoid paying.

I was called by one of the ladies, advised of the situation and had to jump in the car and get over to the hotel as fast as possible before all hell broke out. I get the men to let me into their room and convince them into giving my employees their money and my introduction fee. I told you I had a smart mouth didn't I.

Fortunately for me I managed to get out of all sorts of situations. Quite often I would have to jump in my car and go and get a lady out of a bad situation and for my troubles I have had knives held up against me and gone through varying threatening moments and somehow managed to leave without a scrape and get the ladies out safely with very little back up.

To say this whole situation was mildly out of character of my upbringing could be an understatement. So why was I doing this? Why was I so reckless? I can only think it was because although I had the kids to look after and I would have done anything to keep them safe, I had seen in my younger years what people will do for sex.

I felt worthless and as a young lady on my own as a single parent, I did feel worthless. Perhaps the excitement and the trust the escorts put in me made me feel more worthwhile. I was not making huge amounts of money as the main agency who I franchised for took most of it off me, however I had enough to pay of my poll tax and not allow me to have to go on any more benefits.

So, what did my dad think of this. Well he knew I was up to something, but we didn't really talk about it. I just stopped taking money off him and learned to stand up for myself. It was really on a need to know basis.

How did I move on from this? I had a young lady who decided to take the wallet, passport and money of a rather dangerous client. I had to retrieve it all back for him. As he offered me some lines of coke (which wasn't really an offer but a command) I realised this was not for me anymore.

I had young kids and although I could see I could successfully run a business, I realised the risk in that industry was huge. It was such a huge hassle for me and in that situation if I didn't get this sorted, I may have really put myself in danger. I just wanted out.

I also had to retrieve money from a guy in a house who had refused to pay a girl. He held a knife up to me. I guess that's when I decided I was rather bored of that world. I literally closed off my phones and disappeared.

What was funny is that in the ghetto fabulous world I was living in, were people committed to crime with a sense of pride. I did all this in a very cloak and dagger way. I was totally under everyone's radar. That's how I liked it. I was able to get out with no bother.

When dealing with the women in the agency I was extremely careful to make sure they were not in any trouble. That they were escorts for their own choice. I would have hated to find out that any of these ladies had been forced into that world. I could never understand why people would work for violent pimps who would take all their money off them and beat them.

These ladies should be offered safety not fear. I did have quite often ladies leaving to go back to work or they had promotions in their day job which allowed them to move on. I hope they did move on. I wish them all my love and thank them for giving me an understanding of their work and for enriching my life.

17 Dancing

So, my next plan when I was short of money was to put my skill of dancing to work. I'm sure when my mum and dad sent me to dance classes this isn't the sort of dancing they wanted me to do. But I had two small boys, a part time job and not enough money.

A friend of mine knew a lot of people in the bouncing industry and they introduced me to a lap dancing club. The lady who looked after the girls became a good friend for quite a few years and I danced for about 3 years.

I would drive to the club 3 times a week, dance, not drink take the money I made in tips and drive home. It was easy money. Pumping R&B and hip-hop music. Girls swinging round poles, yeah you know the sort of place. If you've not actually been to one you've probably seen them on films.

The thing that always gets me is that in films these girls are always portrayed as the settings around men's scenes, while men do business. Which I guess is correct from a men's point of view, but from the women who work at these places the men are part of the scenery around their places of work, while they do business.

For the women, the place couldn't be less sexual. They are working to pay their bills, they may be mothers and wives making money from the people who wish to come into their domain. For me that was very apparent. Again, there were some ladies who were vulnerable, but those that weren't were lionesses.

It substituted my part time income and enabled me to buy school uniforms, trainers, holidays etc. for the boys. I did absolutely nothing more than dance. I loved the dancing element. The club was dark and quite dingy, but I had a great time with the women who worked there.

We were such a good team, looking out for one another. You could make a lot of money in tips at Christmas especially. I had a special suitcase with all my dancing clothes and actually had a great time.

Most of the women were again like me just trying to get by although there were a few who seemed to have serious problems. It does grieve me when I hear women who work in the sex industry saying that women are in control, in some cases I agree, but as with anything there will always be vulnerable people who may be being forced into such industries by greedy violent people or drugs.

I saw some of these incidents where clearly some of the women had issues. To a degree I was one of those, although at the time I wouldn't have agreed. But looking back at how things fell apart for me after the incident in Rhodes, as far as my opinion of myself and my body, and perhaps it may have made me choose a route of seeing myself as an object of sex. Perhaps I may not have considered it if that had not happened to me. I am not really sure.

All good things must come to an end and it became time to move on. One day a manager from the place I was working came into the club and basically asked me to go out with him. I said no. He then threatened to tell my employers I had a second job, which he did. I had to go through disciplinary at work, which eventually got dropped as there was nothing in my contract saying I couldn't dance for tips.

Also, they could see that as I was a single parent, and the manager was supposed to be my senior and it wouldn't look good that he had tried to get me sacked for not sleeping with him.

Also, he was also in the club which didn't look great for him to be trying to take the higher moral ground when all I was doing was trying to substitute a very low wage. Just a man thinking he was all powerful. In the end he left. I stayed.

Funny how people stick their necks out for you in such time. One kind male colleague pointed out he fixed cars on the side for tips too, so he couldn't see why I should be in trouble for what I was doing. He saved the day really and I will be forever grateful.

The whole thing did make me very stressed and depressed though and seemed very unfair as I was working so hard to pay for the things my little family needed.

18 My Little house

I did really like my little house. It was 100 years old, but had been refurbished before I bought it, however it had no central heating but had 2 gas fires, one in the front room and one in the back. It was very cold in the winter and hot water bottles were essential. The kitchen units were nice and new, and the bathroom was quite big. It had a nice feel to it.

I decorated and kept it nice painting and decorating it regularly. Dad and my brother laid slabs in the little yard and dad got a shed built and had turf put down, so we had a nice lawn. He made some borders and it wasn't long before the garden was blooming in the way dads' green fingers always made our gardens bloom

Living at this house we had interesting neighbours. The first ones we had were a family which were great. The daughter played with the boys and it all seemed quite nice. On the road I made friends with quite a few people. One of the friends I still know and one I married (and remain married to) . There was another family who I made friends with and they were a bit angry at times. They fell out with the neighbours opposite and fights would break out on the street.

I watched out of my window while the local neighbourhood gathered to watch these events. Kicking of cars, arguments and fights. But once it came to a house break-in, and an attack with an axe. Fortunately, no one was seriously hurt, and the police arrived quickly. There were small children in the house which was sad. It was all about being seen as bad which sounds ridiculous I know.

The family who lived next door moved out and unfortunately a group of young girls moved in with a large appetite for the local gangsters. This had a knock-on effect for us next door. Music got loud and there were lots of comings and goings.

My dad on a couple of occasions went around to ask them to keep the music down as they couldn't even hear the television in our house. I'm so pleased they weren't abusive to him, they didn't turn it down. They held parties late at night with the music so loud we couldn't sleep.

My boys got used to sleeping with earplugs in. Most days there would be groups of people sitting on the little wall outside my house when I would come home from picking the boys up from school, who would make comments under their breath which was quite intimidating. It's a good job I didn't speak back as these people were up to no good. I just quietly went about my business and hatched a plan to get out.

One morning my boyfriend went out to work to find a group of armed police outside the house telling him to go back in. He told them he had to go to work, so they told him to get away fast. As this unfolded, me and my sons watched out the window with school time looming, it seemed they were looking for weapons.

Eventually the police kicked in the door and pulled out the girls. What struck me at this moment was how dysfunctional a section of that street was. The girls were shouting and asking the police why they weren't searching my house or the other houses on the either side of them?

The other neighbour was an 80-year-old woman who lived a humble existence. I doubted she or indeed I would have arms hidden in our houses. But also, the guy who lived opposite decided now was the time, whilst this drama was going on, to do some pull ups on his door frame. This was all a strangely disturbing and dysfunctional scene to wake up too.

Soon after this event a representative of the police asked if I could agree to having a microphone set up in my house to record the bad neighbours. I declined as I felt it may be putting me and my family in danger of reprisal if the neighbours ever found out.

This was the time I decided to leave. I'd had enough. That week I came home from work to find dad and the kids sitting in the living room trying to watch television but having to have ear plugs in again. That was it!! I was worried about us being hurt and not getting any sleep. It was having a big impact on us as a little family.

I dragged the boys around loads of letting agents on a local high Street not having much luck. Apparently being a single mum with two boys was a risk, even if I had a job.

But eventually I found an agency who took me on and we left within the week. I had to just give up my lovely little house, sell it around a year before the house prices rose, which means I left with nothing. But we all got a bit more sleep, which was worth it.

19 The End of a Great Life

Dad had a bad knee which had been gradually bothering him more and more and decided to have an operation. During the operation the surgeons detected Parkinson's and unfortunately dad declined. It was at first gradual but once it set in it moved rapidly. He became shut in his body unable to help himself. He always said this is not what he wanted, but in later life I guess we can't control such things.

I would try and help out as much as I could. At the time I had returned to college, was working full time, and had 2 teenagers, a husband and a very young daughter. It was a tough time. It was also emotionally tough.

To see Parkinson's, take away dad as a person was heartbreaking. I think at first, I thought it would all be ok. But it wasn't. I tried to shut it out and continued my daily calls to him when I was on my lunch hour. He had been sitting in his seat for so long his joints seized up, so even when he was lying in his bed his legs were always bent. He would have been screaming inside and I knew it by the way he looked at us. No one could fix him as much as we all tried. His partner worked so hard with him. I know it was so hard for her. She tried and worked so hard with him.

My brother and I were with him when he passed away. I remember going to see him straight from work. His partner and her friends were there when I arrived, but they left shortly after, knowing I was there to keep him company.

They told me how he seemed quite attentive on that day which was encouraging. I was doing some course work and but when I looked up dad had a strange look to his eyes. I called the nurse and she advised me gently that the time had come. He wouldn't last long.

I called his partner back, but she said she had just got home and would return the next day. I imagine she thought he would be ok as he had shown a little improvement on that day. I'm not sure she understood he was going. I called my brother who was working in Worcester and he said he would jump in his car and drive straight over. It would take him about forty minutes.

I stood by my dad and stroked his hair and hands. I don't know if he knew I was there at all. I was thinking what he would like to hear. It strikes me as quite funny now, and I know if dad was with me now he would think it funny, but I knew he would like singing. But the only thing I could think of to sing was "Come by Yah" so I sang that rather gently to him. I can just picture dad on his death bed thinking "please love, stop it!!"

My brother arrived, and we sat. I told him about my singing and we laughed. I know Dad would have been laughing with us. I think it felt good to share a moment of laughter, even in such a sad time.

I called my dad's sister to tell her the situation and when I went back in the room, held my dad's hand whilst my brother placed his hand on dad's hair, the nurse was with us talking us though the situation, my dad passed away. August 2009.

He always said he wouldn't last long when he stopped teaching, and this was true as he lasted about two years.

Something I remember about my dad at the end was how blue his eyes were. I had never noticed this but in his last moments I was looking into his eyes which had become the color of the sea on a beautiful sunny day. He looked so at peace. I will never forget that moment.

After dad went I felt incredibly empty. It's like I knew he was going but I really didn't think he would. The voice on the end of the phone was gone. I was incredibly busy with my job as a Quantity Surveyor, my college work and my family. But to clear my head I decided to take up something new. I took up fencing.

As in with swords not putting up fences. I met a friend there who is still my friend, who was also doing fencing to take her mind of her father's death too. Life is odd sometimes. It's strange how life brings you new people.

20 Re-education

Re-education has been a huge thing for me. Firstly, as I felt inadequate for not being academic. Secondly, I have needed to educate myself in how to do what I wanted to do. I'm still working on that.

I have had quite a few moments of trying to get rid of the feelings of inadequacy and academic stupidity. I don't think my parents and peer groups meant to make anyone feel like that, but the perception for me whilst growing up was academia was the key to a happy and full life.

So, after failing at school as I found absolutely no inspiration or aspiration for my future. I mean whatever I wanted to do I probably couldn't. I was told I was either going to be a secretary or nurse or teacher, which is fine but wasn't something that inspired me.

I've always thought what a big world we have with huge opportunities so there must be something else out there for me. So, I decided to re-educate. This happened slowly.

First in the early 2000s I put myself on a counselling course. It was 3 months long and I loved it. I found I could do all the assignments and at times challenging, but I completed it.

Next, I decided dad valued people who knew history, being a history teacher. I thought I should ease myself in slowly so decided to do an Open University Living Arts course.

I listened to Vaughan Williams who I loved. Again, I completed it with ease. The next course I did was a year level 3 course "certificate in Humanities". This was brilliant! I learnt about the Enlightenment. I read and wrote about philosopher's like Jean-Jacques Rousseau, Voltaire and the Marque de Sade, which was interesting indeed.

The latter a bit disturbing at times. Then the French Revolution. Liberty, Equality, Fraternity! I enjoyed it so much and got good results. It was challenging, but that's a good thing.

I stopped there for a while as I had suitably impressed my dad who realised that I was rather bright after all, and to be fair I wasn't that bothered after all when he said he was proud of me, as I had grew to realise if I applied myself I could do anything.

I decided after storming out of a job (I will explain that in a later chapter) that I would quite fancy going into the building industry. I had learnt a lot of things about property from my dad, so I thought it may be a good idea to go and learn something in a more professional manor.

I called Birmingham University and asked for course advice saying I wanted to work somehow professionally within the building trade. They suggested I go on a BTec in Construction and the Built environment and follow it up with an HNC, then go to University.

It seemed like a rather long process, but I thought it was going to be a worthwhile one. I called the local college and enrolled myself on a day a week BTec Course.

It was great. I met the only female to be in the class on the second week of me being there and we had a fantastic time together. I managed to also get my job as a trainee surveyor to fit round the course, so was getting paid for a week's work with one day leave for my college.

I did well at the BTec so moved on the HNC. I made a new friend there who I still see now, though him being a customer of mine for the company I work for selling into Social Housing.

We had some good laughs through those years and probably more than my companions I found this course actually changed my life for the better. I realised I could actually achieve good marks and found a voice for myself in education.

It was a huge confidence boost for me. I remember getting a drawing board put in front of me for the first time and being told to draw up some plans, I immediately said I couldn't, but in the weeks to come I really enjoyed doing this and totally turned my can't do that attitude into a "ok let's have a go" attitude.

I still actually visit the college what gave me all that opportunity with the company I work for, giving presentations to the electrical apprentices and students. I love it when I see a spark in one of the student's eyes and when I tell them how I had come from not so good a place but had grasped learning with both hands and it had changed my life. I'm truly grateful for those lecturers who believed in me.

21 Jobs

My job history goes far back. After school my mum and dad thought I may be good at beauty therapy. I had looked after my skin very well as I had suffered so badly with eczema. I went along with it as I wasn't sure what else I could actually do as my expectation of my potential were low.

So, I started beauty college. This was short lived, and I couldn't apply myself. I enjoyed it all at the start and was quite enthusiastic, but my weed smoking was getting more regular and I lost interest in being a beauty therapist. I also looked at the pay scale and decided it wouldn't give me the life I actually wanted. So with this in mind, I went on the dole until I could find something that may bring me more money.

My parents scoffed when I told them but had to let me get on with it as I advised them my brother was unemployed and he was happy. They must have been quite disappointed, but to be fair during my time out I did do some work as I get bored very easily.

So, going onto jobs I've done. I've not put all these on my CV as there just isn't enough time. I can imagine some calls from previous employers on this.

1/Job at a big toy shop and I hated it. They made me dress up as a teddy bear and stand by the Thomas the Tank Engine stand. I had to listen to the Thomas theme tune over and over again. It drove me mad. I did get promoted to 'The party Shop' where I would occasionally have to dress up as a rag doll. My self-esteem was so low at this point I would generally drink on a lunch time then spend the whole day staggering around drunk inside a bear outfit looking for somewhere to sit down.

2/ I worked in a butchers, for about 1 year. Hated it and left. The lad that worked there kept advising me he was on more money than me because he was male and therefore he could tell me what to do. Totally unfair and couldn't work like that. He brought out violent feelings in me due to his consistent bullying, which wasn't great when surrounded by sharp knives.

3/Child-minding, wasn't really my thing. I felt forced into it by my parents. It gave me too much time to think and thinking wasn't a good thing at that time.

4/ Secretary. Walked out when I was asked to wear a short skirt and suspenders, as the boss had important customers in and the boss thought it would be nice to see me like that when I brought in the tea and coffee. Unbelievable. Quite funny too as my parents although they accepted it did seem to not 100% believe me. Probably due to my bad work record and I seemed to attract the attentions of pervy guys. Like that was my fault?

It was after that job I found out I was pregnant, dad left, mum died, and I had a baby. I took a break after all that happening in short succession

Jobs After my son was born and after I had lost mum.

1/ Bar staff in busy pub. Lunchtimes only. I used to walk the big drinkers up to the next pub which was open longer before I went home. They appreciated someone to help them on their way and had the tendency to wander or talk to strangers in the street. We all held hands up the road to avoid anyone getting lost. Kind of like sheep herding I think.

2/Secretary at electrical company not worthy of too much mention, although I hated every moment. Don't think they liked me. I just couldn't get my head around the old-style switchboard so kept cutting people off. Probably not the best for business.

3/ Cashier at bookies. Actually, quite liked this job. Very busy and full of action as it was in the centre of Birmingham. I had a fortunate incident one Christmas whilst doing this job and was particularly skint. One of the customers gave me a couple of carrier bags full of spirits, whiskey, vodka, Bacardi and rum to hold behind the counter for him which I did.

But then within moments the police came in and arrested him. I waited a few days to see if he would return but was advised by one of his mates that he had been sent to prison and not to expect to see him again for a couple of years. I was living in shared accommodation at this time and returned home a hero with those bags. I can tell you that those bottles of spirit really made that Christmas a much merrier one for us all.

4/Tarot Reader. This I did as a bit of a joke. Worthy story too so I will detail. I saw the advert in the evening mail. I applied, I went and purchased some tarot cards and I blagged it. We took phone calls and did readings for people. In the next room there were ladies doing the sex lines. They didn't have videos at this time, so it was all done by phone.

Which was a good thing because if the customers had seen them all in their leisure gear, all sorts of ages sizes, levels of cleanliness with fags hanging out of their mouths they may not have been on the phone for long. As I found out later, men can be easily fooled. They used to sit banging whips off tables making sounds of joy whilst looking uninterested.

I basically used to take the calls and then just lay out cards and read the cards from what I saw. It's quite easy and everyone seemed happy, until one day the manager called me into the office and asked me "are you a witch?"

At first, I thought he said "are you my bitch?" and wondered if he was trying to get me to move over to the sex line. But no, he was actually asking if I was indeed a witch. I just stared at him for a while and said I didn't think I was one, however surely it would be a great benefit to be one in such a job. He said no because he didn't trust witches and I clearly was one, so I should get my things and leave.

To be honest I have had bosses say weird things over the years, but this will always stand out as one of the best stupid boss things that I have ever had the pleasure to hear.

I may actually write about stupid things said at work at some point. It seems to be quite a thing at work for people to actually go to find something stupid to have an issue with.

Maybe to get rid of you because they are intimidated by you and they are concerned you could take over their job, I just don't know but this has to be at the top of the stupid list. And for the record, I'm not a witch, I don't think I am anyway.

5/ Advertising sales. This was a cold calling job where you go through the phone book calling businesses and trying to get them to advertise in a random and not highly used paper. It was dreadful. I stormed out in such a huff leaving a hair extension on the floor and having to go back in and retrieve it.

I had 2 other similar jobs like this, one for a rave magazine where the promoter at a rave I was reviewing, showed me his penis for no particular reason, wasn't sure if I should hit it with my Filofax but settled on asking him if he wanted me to include it in the review of the club.

He put it away and apologised. The other one was just ridiculous. One of those places when you had to run up and down the office ringing a bell when you got a sale. It was the days when you could smoke at work, so we worked away in a haze of smoke, because everyone was so stressed with their jobs the level of smoking was increased.

A couple of months in they decided that all the smokers should stand in the corner of the office to smoke. The trouble with that is that most people smoked, so we all ended up in the corner of the office in a haze of smoke instead, which just eventually just drifted over the office anyway.

They were so vile to the staff they would get everyone in a team meeting first thing in the morning and say "if you don't want to be here just go now". They used to lose about half of the staff on a daily basis, then some new agents would start a couple of days later. Huge turnover of staff. Inevitably one day I just though "sod this" and left too. It was quite a relief to be honest.

6/ Running a promotion agency. As previously mentioned.

7/ Complaints handler. I learned a lot from this job. The complaints were so harsh and abusive we were allowed to read magazines and books. I read a lot during this time, most memorably American Psycho by Bret Euston Eliot. Quite appropriate for some of the calls. But seriously, I learned how to let customers blow off steam, apologise to them and then find solutions for them. It was a hugely useful thing to learn. Also, I wanted to get them sorted as fast as possible so I could get on with my book!

8/ Customer services in a building society. Again, learning different roles from customer services to collections and commercial accounts. I was there for a fair bit of time and although very poorly paid I learnt a huge amount.

9/Pole dancing as discussed.

10/Trainee Quantity Surveyor. I felt right proper in this job. Like I'd made it for a short while. My role was to look after the gas and pluming engineers for a large Maintenance Contractor. I had to provide valuations on the work done at the end of the month. Manage a small office where I was so lucky to have some wonderful ladies working with me, and take day to day responsibility of sick leave, annual leave etc.

I mucked in and I did my very best to learn as much as I could. I never really saw myself as a manager, I just took care of everyone the best I could and led from the front. I learnt my trade. It wasn't until my colleagues would point me out as the manager, I realised they saw me as that. I thought we were just working as a team, but I was leading them without realising it. I was made redundant as were all of the company after a few years as the company fell on troubled times. It was 2010 and jobs were scarce, so I took a side step.

11/Trade price Estimator. For this role I was literally sitting by a computer working out prices and profit margins on items for building. It was incredibly boring, and I used to sit and make up songs and basically disrupt the team as much as I could. One day the national social housing sales manager sat next to me.

I asked if I could have a word and we went into a meeting room. I told him I was wasted in the role and should be in front of his customers. He liked the fact I had gone up to ask him that, so at the first opportunity he got me on his team.

Sadly, the day he gave me a job, he advised me he was moving to work with the customer I would be looking after. He was the boss who never was, but we get together now and then, have a giggle and put the world to rights. He is another person I feel grateful to. The sales manager and the customers Procurement Director were also fantastically supportive and believed in me. Gratitude to you all. Bet you never guessed I would be writing a book.

12/Sales, I have always enjoyed account managing. National account managing took me out on the open road to places I hadn't been to before and meeting lots of new people. It's a great job for me and I see women doing so well in this sort of role. It's funny as when I was a school it was seen as 'salesman' which was not considered a job many women seemed to do.

I'm sure there were a few pioneering women sales reps out there in the 1980s, but it wasn't so highlighted. It was certainly never given to me as an option when I was looking at careers. I have to say though, if you are a female and looking for a role where you can grow in confidence, a job which will be fairly flexible both ways but also give you something different every day, this job would suit you most definitely.

I would be looking after a number of big national accounts supplying their products through a national wholesale distribution. I would be managing the commercial side, pricing etc. but most importantly building relationships. The relationship part is the area that fits me the most.

I would get to do monthly meetings with the customer, or more if they required, meeting their regional managers, making sure everything was running smoothly and they were happy and not wanting to move to another wholesaler. We would work on tenders to retain their business and work to fix any problems which may arise.

I may be out on the road all week or sometimes a few days then be at home working on commercials and getting up to date on admin on other days. I would build relationships with our branches to make sure they had all the support they needed to service the customers.

There were ups and downs in this job. Total rollercoaster. You have to take the lows but really enjoy the highs.

I would take the customers out for meals and events, horse racing and all sorts of other events. We would work on trade shows which would be exhausting as you would be spending 8 hours on a stand representing the company by day, then taking customers out in the evening and getting back very late and rather tipsy, then have to get up in a few hours and do the same again. Had some great nights out with colleagues and customers alike. Great memories which still make me laugh.

Really believe in this job I made friends for life. We still chat now and then and catch up when we can. I also learned to work with different levels of people. From office, branch staff to MDs and CEOs.

What I realised from this sort of work was that I'm good at what I do. I am able to tap into people and help them with what they need. One of my customers told me "I see many reps, but you don't give it the big talk, you listen, I sometimes don't always understand, but I go away and come back with what I need. I trust you." Trust is very important when looking after customers.

As a Rep, you need to stand out. The customer needs to trust you and want to see you, hopefully like you too. It's always nice to have a nice meal and drink with a good customer knowing they want to work with you.

Also, when you hear they are so supportive of you and offer references. I can say it has been a great confidence boost to me working with some wonderful senior managers who have had great belief in me. Hopefully if they read this they will know who they are, and I thank them for helping me build my belief in myself and helping me lift myself after feeling I was useless. It meant so much to me and helped me on my journey.

I'm still in sales as I write this book. Within my growth in this industry, I have found the areas where I have needed development and in my current role I was certainly thrown out my comfort zone. Very soon after starting, I was giving the companies presentation in front of 200 people at a tech talk.

I have continued to work and present in front of people with growing crowds, along with my colleagues around the country who are doing the same.

I'm currently working regionally, and I have to get our product on the Specification of our customers. So it's relationship building, planning and strategy. I do love it though. Seeing our customers and training people. I will go into colleges and to our customers and various associations to deliver presentations.

Presenting was something I never thought I could do. I had always asked for support on this but not achieved it until I moved to this job. It's tough standing in front of people and talking if you're not used to it. I was so scared the first time, but I do it regularly now along with my colleagues over the UK.

I have presented in front of small and large crowds. Again, what's been important in this role is having great supportive colleagues and management. I'm truly blessed. I still have a lot of improvement and need to grow in this area, but it is another string to my bow and a wonderful thing to connect to lots of people. Maybe one day I will be presenting my story.

If you're nice, but firm and competent and prepared to put in some long shifts, you can do well in this world. Focus and self-discipline is very important. With all the jobs I've had, there is always an element of people trying to make things more complicated than things need to be. Just get on with the business and try and avoid the politics.

I've also had people that have not been happy that I have had my own mind and took opportunities. You will find that if you are curious and ask for things in life they come to you a lot easier than if you just sit there and wait to be recognised. This is something I've really experienced and witnessed.

Sales jobs can be a massive high but also a massive low. You can earn some fantastic money if you hit your targets and can work with some amazingly driven people. My experience of successful teams have been ones where the managers are part of the team.

When it becomes a "them an us" atmosphere within a sales team, there can be problems with staff retention. If you understand each other's strengths, some may be technical, some may be analytical, some may be networkers (I fall into the networking category) you can all draw on each other to create a wonderful team.

And with the management working with you as opposed to against you, the sales magic can really happen. It can be very long hours and I have seen many people fall sick, mentally and physically due to the stress. It's really not always for everyone.

22 Return of the Biological Family

I had always wondered about my biological family. Growing up I had dreamt about who they might be. It never really bothered me too much though as a child as I was so happy and cared for. I do remember one time at school, primary school when I told someone I was adopted, and they told someone else and before long everyone knew. Kids can be cruel.

By lunchtime the class had decided that they weren't my friend as I was adopted. This didn't really last long though because I had some really loyal friends and I was charismatic and was able to turn it around, and they all forgot they were supposed to be not be my friend and we moved on.

It has stayed in my memory though and I remember thinking that I must be a bit different at the time.

I had discussed it with my brother from time to time and he had said he wasn't really that fussed. It may have been a loyalty thing perhaps but in time we would both retrace our biological families.

My brother and I also have mentioned that there was no time in our childhood that our parents ever made us feel we weren't theirs biologically. I really don't think mum and dad could have loved us more if we were.

But strangely in the end it was a moment that came to me. When I was about to get married (the first time) I had to get a birth certificate. I couldn't find one, with all the moving around I had very little of anything so I had to call the council to get one. When I did I was asked if I wanted my birth certificate or my adopted one.

After a pause, I opted for both. I was advised to get the adopted one, I would have to have to see someone from their adoption team. I had become quite intrigued at this point but decided to wait a while as I had a lot going on, so I would have the adopted certificate.

I then got married, had a baby and then got divorced (yeah ok a quick turnaround) but once I had a moment to rethink the matter I revisited that option. I ordered my Original Birth Certificate and I was advised I had to pick up the certificate from a counsellor.

At that time if you were adopted before 1970 you had to see a counsellor. The counsellor went through all sorts of information and scenarios that could happen in the process of finding lost parents. Some of which I remember.

- How would you feel if you are rejected?
- What if they have new families and none of them know?
- What if they are tramps? (interesting one)
- What if they are dead?
- How will you cope if they are drug addicts and think you can fund their habits? (I hoped not)

There were other ones, but those are the ones that stuck with me. I just said I owe them nothing if one of those situations were to happen, so I would walk away.

To be fair I think I would have. I wasn't really feeling a requirement to have a mum and dad at that point and I was just curious to fit the pieces of my personal jigsaw into place. The counsellor gave me my certificate and there was two names, mother and father and an address of where my mother's family had lived at the time of my birth. Straight away with the information to hand I wanted to investigate. It was a very exciting feeling for me.

The counsellor advised me that if I find anything out to let her know and she would make the first contact. It was quite easy as I called directory enquiries, who advised me there was still someone of that name living under the same address and they gave me a phone number.

I passed this onto the counsellor who called me back to tell me that this was the address of my mother's father, my paternal grandfather and a message had been sent to my mother and the counsellor as expecting a call from her.

It was a bit of a waiting game then. But shortly I had a call from the counsellor to say she had spoken to my mother and she would be happy to talk to me. I should phone her at 8pm that night. Wow...

I sat there with a phone number in my hand for some time. I had to wait about 5 hours before I could phone. It was weird as I look back, as my emotions over the years had been so pushed to the limits but I remember being very calm.

The clock hit 8pm and I picked up the phone. She had a soft Southampton voice and we spoke for some time, and again a week later. She explained why I was given up for adoption and she had suffered terrible guilt and heartbreak for doing so. I won't go into her story as it's not mine to tell.

I went to meet her for the first time soon after our first call. I caught a train from Birmingham to Southampton. I remember thinking if I don't like her I can just catch the train back. But as I drew up to Southampton station, I saw a lady standing waiting on her own who looked very similar to me.

We didn't throw ourselves at each other in an emotional embrace like in the movies. We looked at each other, smiles and said hello. I probably was staring at her loads. The only full blood members of my family I had seen were my sons. So, it was incredible to see a female who had such similarities to me. We went back to hers and sat and talked. We had dinner and the next day I met my two sisters.

One of my sisters is the same mother and the other is the same mother and father. It was a good reunion and we have all kept in touch since. I don't see them as much as I would like to due to the distance but also the work and family commitments of all of us. I hope in the future we will see more of each other.

My biological dad reunion was more of a surprise. It was a few months after my dad had passed away and I was sitting in my office at work as a Trainee Quantity Surveyor. I was remarried, and the boys were growing nicely. I now had a daughter who was about 4 at this time. I was checking my email and I noticed I had one from my biological mother telling me I had another sister on my biological dads' side and she was looking for me.

I called her, and she gave me my sisters name and said she was on Facebook and if I wanted to speak to her I would be very welcome. Obviously, I did, curious as always. We talked and got on well. She told me my biological father lived in Spain and he would like to talk to me too. It was not long before I got to speak to him too.

He was due over to England. So, my husband and I went down to meet them in Southampton. We stayed overnight in a local hotel and then in the morning sat inside a waited for them. My husband was asking how I was feeling to be meeting my biological father.

Again, I was calm. I said I would take it in my stride and if we liked them we would have a lovely time, if we didn't we could jump in the car and go back home. As it happened we liked them. Again, there was lots of looking at each other.

We went over to my sister's house for a BBQ and some get to know each other time. I had a migraine from the excitement of it all and had to have a lie down. Well it was a lot to take in. I may not show huge emotions, but my body certainly has a way of showing it in the form of migraines. Thanks for that!

We have since had visits down to my sister and to see my dad in Spain. My sons have also been to visit their grandad in Spain. He has been over here with his wife too.

This for me has been a good experience. I've been lucky to have had the opportunity to have been brought up by wonderful parents and to have had the opportunity to meet my biological parents.

Both are very different and my feelings for both sets are different. I think initially I had a feeling I was perhaps being disloyal to my adopted parents, but I don't think they would have seen it like that.

The parents I knew and grew up with were kind and I think they would have just wanted me to be happy. If they had both been around now, would I have made those connections? Who knows? What I do know is that we have all, myself and my children, been able to fit a missing part to the jigsaw.

23 Counselling and Coaching

I have always been an advocate for finding help when you need it. I have had so many situations where I have required some sort of support.

The lack of conversations available about certain subjects with my parents led me to have my first counselling with the Rape Crisis. Although I did give a false name, I did feel it quite natural to go and tell someone who seemed like a responsible adult about my situation and it gave me some comfort.

I didn't do it enough back then but have revisited it on that and many situations which I truly believe led back to that one situation in Rhodes.

I have gone to counselling to get me off smoking weed. That took some time as there were issues around my requirement to self-medicate so I needed to dig deep to completely shake off that addiction.

However, on that subject like I stated before I'm totally for the uses of medical marijuana. However, the way I was using it was throwing me further into depression and leading me to not face my issues full on.

I have worked though my "Why" I thought it was ok to set up an escort agency, and to my lack of self-worth and buying into the fact I was just a visual thing for men, which led me to lap dancing. I'm not saying this is why all people lap dance and run escort agencies, but it was my reason.

I didn't think I could do anything else and by helping myself out financially I thought my highest worth was at the service of men. This is about my reasoning and I'm not talking for everyone else's. Just in case someone wants to get into an argument about my opinion.

I honestly think that if I had not gone and found counselling I would not have gone to college and found my way and worth. I've not reached all my goals yet and I find that counselling helps me reflect logically and come to terms with things. I have also had couples counselling when having marriage problem. I would recommend this, however you both need to be willing and open minded to make this worthwhile.

Coaching has been something that has been quite new to me. I started coaching about 6 months ago. I decided I wasn't sure which way to take my career and I also have a 50th Birthday coming up in a years' time and was having a massive wobble in all areas of my life.

I had watched Ange Loughran on Social Medial for some time and knew she would be someone I could work with. I was right. It's been and continues to be an amazing journey, and I now have positive thoughts for the future me.

Surrounding myself with such positivity and having someone who really sees my potential and helps me tap into the best me I can be, is such a wonderful thing. I would like to help others feel this.

I know that some of us hit our 50's thinking we can wind down now, but I know women who are in their late 80's and still living active lives. My thought was what do I want to do that will be able to contribute better in my older years and to be a better version of myself?

Although I have written on and off, I doubt I would have been confident enough to get on with this book without Ange Loughran's encouragement. I've become even more inquisitive and curious by reading more and listening to audio books, firstly recommended to me, then moving onto things I am finding for myself.

I will be looking to coach and help people, on the way those like her have helped me and many others find the best in themselves. I would wholeheartedly encourage you as a reader to find help when you need it. I wish I had of had better guidance earlier.

It's fantastic to see groups of women supporting each other and for me encouraging me to tell my story.

During this process I have learnt so much about how people can do amazing things to help others with coaching and counselling, and this has really given me a sense of hope for the future.

Also seeing how I can help others too has been incredibly inspiring. I'm not as financially successful as some, I'm not a top business owner. I have however overcome my own traumas and bad decisions which could have been life changing in totally the wrong direction.

There was always the two voices in my head, one was telling me I was worthless and I may as well dance naked for guys, the other was telling me I could do wonderful things. I'm glad to say that fortunately the voice telling me I could do great things has eventually won.

I'm not done yet though. I'm sure there are loads more things I can do. When I recently told my coach, I felt like at my age I may have missed the boat, she told me I can't have missed it when I was just getting on it, which I loved. I'm coming up to 50 and now I see a big future ahead.

24 Thoughts on work

As I never really knew what I wanted to do in life I did drift. I still am at nearly 50. I can remember thinking "what am I doing?" in the last few years of working in the bank, and that was 12 years ago. I have worked with some amazing people though in my career and keep in touch with many of them still. Mainly my experience of colleagues had been really good.

I have laughed with colleagues and cried with them.

I really thought going into the construction industry would be a good thing for my daughter to see. It was something I would have struggled to do when I was young as it wasn't the sort of industry girls went into.

There are a huge amount of opportunities these days for women. Still not enough women going to college to study in the construction industry which I would like to see more. I do see the occasional woman when I'm training electricians, but not as many as I would like. There are lots more now in supply sales and wholesaling I think.

I watched senior managers and what they did and how they did it as a study. I came to the realisation that they were no better than me and that really if you put your mind to something you can do it within reason.

Obviously, you have to put in a lot of hard work and change your habits. There is no way I would have achieved my goals so far if I was still smoking the whacky baccy. Although I'm sure there are many bosses who do. Who knows?

Theses Senior managers may have just taken different paths to me, well in all honesty most people did. Obviously, I went down a more obscure path than most to put it mildly. I had not ever applied for any senior roles, it wasn't that I couldn't do it. Maybe as a single parent I could not have committed the time or may have felt unworthy of such a role when I was younger.

At one place I worked at, the senior managers thought very highly of themselves and their status, which would baffle me as they were only humans, and with the knowledge of some guys in power from running the agency. I'm sure at times some of them may have been less human than most.

Sometimes at Christmas there would be a sign on the wall saying "celebrity balloon race" the so-called celebs were the senior managers who worked on the top floor, they would grace us with their company. We in the office were mainly women and they would play the balloon race with us.

No Hands…. Passing the balloon body to body. You just couldn't make it up. When I look back it was so ridiculous. And who had decided that these people were celebrities? I would always hope they had Brad Pitt hidden in the office and he was going to come down to play, but no, the senior celeb managers.

I had a conversation with a colleague recently about the idea of opportunity. He was asking why I had not gone for many senior roles. The only reason is that I just hadn't, and if I had, perhaps I would have got one eventually by gaining experience in the interview and selection stage.

He pointed out that I had the experience and especially when it came to people, more than a lot of senior managers. Again, those in higher positions aren't there necessarily because they are better, just that they have applied for the roles. We've all known totally rubbish managers, more good ones in my case thankfully apart from my earlier days in work.

I can count the inspirational ones on one hand which doesn't say much as I've worked for loads of managers. These managers have just applied for the jobs. And maybe the reason why there are so many bad ones is that the good people just don't apply for the roles. Again, these are just observations of my experience in work. Yours may be very different.

Quite a few older men in my life have generally took it on themselves to try and knock me down a peg or two. I remember when I was training for my HNC I told one of my father's friends and he told me that I should forget about doing something like that, it wouldn't be for me.

If I had of listened to the nay sayers I would have had to stay at home and try and rely on someone to take care of me. I'm not sure why this has been suggested to me through my life as I'm clearly not the sort of woman who is waiting to be taken care of. It still happens. I can take banter all day and give it back but as I'm coming up to 50 I can't understand why a certain type of male still wants to go into father mode on me. It's quite bizarre.

I go back to a time when my dad in a fit of rage told me that I would infuriate men in my lifetime for my lack of obedience. I know years later he would have cringed to discuss this conversation, but it was something I have always remembered.

Why do I have to be obedient? I am able to support myself, I have made it that way. Ok I'm not great with money but I can get out and make it certainly. It's odd because later in me and my dad's relationship, he said I should come to terms with who I am and be proud of myself. I have done this, and it was great advice from Dad.

Many a time have I had senior men (age and position) trying to analyse me. They love it. Sometimes because of a job position there is a presumption that they are much wiser then I or anyone who works below them.

Which is fine, if that makes them happy to think that. People can be more educational or experienced in some areas and in some things but I'm sure that goes for all of us. We all have specialities and strengths and it's learning to use them to our advance and to the service of helping others.

It has been said that I am a nonconformist and a free spirit. It has been said I may never find happiness. Maybe that's true. I've worked very hard at being a free spirit and a nonconformist. I'm proud of that, and happiness? maybe I will never find true happiness, however I will continue my life in pursuit of it.

I was driving home recently listening to a podcast by Rob Moore, "The disruptive Entrepreneur" where he was talking about the same thing. Along the lines of people thinking you should only do what makes you happy. His thoughts were that you can't always do what makes you happy, it's not a given.

If we were all happy all of the time we would get nothing done. The pursuit of happiness is what sets people to action. I totally agree with this. I'm not saying I'm unhappy, I'm just still finding my happy place, and in the pursuit, hopefully I will help a few people along the way. Try Robs Podcasts, they are great. Especially when you spend your time driving!

25 Strong Words

"Hate is a very strong word", My mum used to say that when I said I hated things. Sprouts, homework tiding my bedroom etc.

I don't hate people. I hate what people do to other people though. I hate murder, mugging, rapes, wars, famines, slavery and genocide. I wish those who performed such vile acts on society were not able to do these things. I guess the majority of us feel that way.

Things that have personally happened to me have not left me filled with hate. I remember a someone saying how I must hate the lady my dad left my mum for. She couldn't understand my lack of hate. I was sad that in the last year of my mum's life she felt great sorrow and heartbreak, but my dad caused that, and I couldn't hate him.

My relative seemed to not understand the forgiveness and peace I had found with the situation, and that my only concern was my dad's wellbeing whilst he was ill. Strange as she was Christian, and doesn't Christian belief hold forgiveness in its core?

The man who raped me, I don't feel hate either. I'm not 100% sure what I feel.... indifferent perhaps? I'm glad I don't hate as I think that may be an all-encompassing thing. I feel if I was to let myself hate I could become the sort of person who commits the sort of human act I dislike.

I wish bad people would just stop it though. I really do! If I had a super power I would like it to make all the people stop doing damage to others go away, so we could all live-in peace without hate. I'm dreaming I know and obviously I don't have the answer.

I wonder if something happened to my nearest and dearest if I would then become so consumed with hate I would turn bad, or would I forgive and try to make better happen? I hope I will never have that choice to make.

What I do think is hugely important, is that I try to make a positive difference to people. I can't change the whole world but if I try to make positive moves to help and look to improve myself which may have the effect of helping those around me, and in the wider world hopefully one day. Start off small I think.

The things that happened to me in my lifetime made me grow as a person and become more determined to do well in life. From being at the bottom of the pile, although I am not a millionaire and still learning, it has allowed me to be able to support myself well without having to resort to any dodgy ways of earning money. It has also given me a great gift of being able to meet lots and lots of people and be able to learn that I can work as well in this world as anyone.

It also shows what a wonderful opportunity we have in this country. It really is true if you put your mind to learning something and set your goals you can achieve them. Why not?? I used to hear people saying that 'if I can do it you can 'but I brushed if off as nonsense. I know now, you can if you want to. I used to self-limit myself because of what other thoughts that I could and couldn't do. I won't be doing that again.

26 Determination and Recovery

I think I have always had a determined streak in my personality. Like I said in an earlier chapter my "I will if you won't let me" attitude had probably made me push away all the negative comments and feelings that have come my way. The more people have put me down, the more I have pushed back.

My daughter recently looked at one of her reports and saw that the teacher had marked her lower than she had expected for her projected GCSE exams, which are still quite a few years away for her. She had a look of determination on her face and said, "I will do better than that, I will prove the teacher wrong." I'm sure she will.

It's this using someone's opinion of you to draw a positive which I think shows great strength and resilience. Many a time when I've been told to be patient, take my time, that's not for you, I've felt deflated.

But what comes from that initial feeling has been what's driven me on. I'm not at my full potential yet I know, but I keep moving towards it.

I know there are lots of people that have had far worse situations. We all suffer loss in life. I miss my mum and dad every day. I don't know how I would cope if I lost a child, I know people who have and seen them bravely carry on. You see it on the telly where people have spoken when they have had family members murdered, they say they forgive the murders, I think they do have such courage.

Clearly as humans we have a huge sense of survival. I think for my situation, closeness of the rape, my mother dying and having a child under such circumstances were hugely challenging situations for me. However, I have not let them define me. It's no excuse for anything that I may have done which may be seen as questionable, however, low self-esteem was the major issue for me in many cases.

Once I got over that, I was able to see the potential. What strikes me now is how lucky I have actually been. I struggled when the boys were little, we may as a family have suffered a bit of first world poverty, but nothing life threatening or anything like we see in the third world. I appreciate and see first-hand how things have got tougher over the past few years for many people in this country and goodness knows what the future will be like. Let's hope we can find better ways to work together to help some of the social issues we face.

I made some crazy decisions but often wonder if I had of had the right people around me at the time, maybe the speed and thought I put into an escort agency could have been focused in a much better way.

You're probably going to be thinking that throughout all of these experiences I've been quite hard and non-emotional. I must have been quite a badass to run an escort agency, well you are mistaken. It was all an act.

I've become more balanced as I've got older and much stronger. When I was younger I was good at putting up a front. I learned to look strong, and interestingly once I started in business I realised that people can be quite critical and expect you to be pragmatic about it   rather than emotional about it. I found it most difficult at the beginning to take criticism and not get upset by it.

I find this a strange thing really as I had been criticised by people I knew for most of my life and to a degree used it to fight back. Once I found people who didn't know me well criticising me I was a little shook up. I can remember being brought to tears on a few occasions and having to excuse myself from meetings to pull myself back together.

In time I've learned from this. I can listen now to criticism and take what I find valid and leave what I don't agree with, importantly, without getting upset. I'm by no means perfect and I'm sure I will be criticised and put down a lot more in my life. Not everyone is going to like me either (although this is hard for me to believe).

Sometimes people criticise you and put you down because of their own agenda, perhaps they are protecting their own position or perhaps the problem is something in them, so they try to bring you down to their level. It's always best to be aware of this but if you feel the criticism is just, then learn from it.

When I was running my agency, I wasn't hard, I was acting out a role in the way I thought it should be played. Looking back, I know that was a very dangerous game to play. I came up against some very dangerous and threatening people but was fortunate enough to be able to use my wits and my common sense to get through some rather tricky situations. I'm lucky I did.

I have learned a lot from people in all areas of business and can now be myself in meetings without having to act anymore. I have realised I am my best asset. My personality is what draws people to me. I'm open and trustworthy. I work well and enjoy sales as people like me so will give me time. They know I will try my best for them and that I am sincere.

Sometimes when I sit in meetings with customers or when I'm presenting I think about how far I've come. I also sometimes wonder if I'm an intruder as I was never expected to do much in life. So maybe there is still an aspect of me that still wants to self-limit. As a child, if I would tell my parents of a goal which they didn't share they would tell me it was a pipe dream and it would never happen.

That was their perception of what was achievable to them, perhaps they had put limits against their achievements? I have tried all my life not to self-limit and dream big and got told that it's unrealistic to do so.

The more I learn, and my confidence grows the less I self-limit. I've achieved things that my parents would have thought was pipe dream, but I know even with the blips and wobbles I've had, they would be proud of me now. After all I am only human.

I mentioned earlier that my mum said I was like the little girl with the curl as child. I've been thinking a lot about the child version of me and I know I wasn't a stroppy kid. I did however have a smart mouth and would be very cutting in very few words.

I always liked the last word, my husband would say I still do, but my poor mum and dad would have more than likely fell victim to this. Also, I was very uncomfortable with my skin and quite often on hefty antihistamine tablets, so I may have been tetchy at times.

You know, when I look back at me as a child, I did feel like a pain in the ass to my parents. The care they had to give me with my skin must have been dreadfully hard work for them. I felt awful and sore most of the time. I used to imagine in my head if I wasn't a human what would I be? If I closed my mind I used to see mud. When I thought about my brother, I used to see light.

Clearly, I had a terrible self-image. I can remember me, and my brother were given a small bit of garden to care for. My brothers' bit was in the light and mine was in the shade. I'm sure my parents didn't intentionally do that, but as my brother's flowers blossomed mine withered and died.

So, I pulled all his flowers out when no one was looking. The little girl with the curl I think. Obviously, I got into trouble and rightly so. It's funny though as far as a child's perception is concerned. In my mind my brother was the favourite, what's interesting is that my brother thought I was the favourite.

In reality both of us were loved the same. But squeezing my eyes closed and seeing myself as mud, I think perhaps a psychologist could have a field day on me with that one.

But in reality most of the time I was pleasant and happy go lucky but could change into a smart ass very fast. Perhaps I'm still the little girl with a curl.

27 Changing

So, I'm coming up to my 50th next year and I guess this is why it was so important to talk about my experiences at this point. I'm changing. I can see it happening to my friends too.

My body has been constantly playing tricks on me over the past few years. I can stand in the mirror each day and see a different me. Sometimes I'm happy with what I see, sometimes I'm critical.

Since having my last child and more recently coming into peri menopause my breasts are like huge udders and my back holds fat more than it ever did. I work out now very regularly, whereas before this year it was more sporadic.

I can get totally obsessive about my scales and have to make sure I put them away so I'm not jumping on them 10 times a day and getting upset with myself for storing an extra pound.

I'm never going to be my 30year old body again. I do realise that but coming to terms with my body at half a century is a battle for me. I have a sweet tooth, and love chocolate, but I count calories to a degree and try my best to eat healthy.

Unfortunately, a job on the road does not always compliment a healthy diet. Stopping at service stations for a sandwich and eating out and drinking with customers is quite cultural in sales.

However, I'm more determined now to make myself a strong healthy woman in my 50's. Not a 30-year-old version of me. The 50-year-old version of me. Strong and maybe carrying a few war wounds but grateful that my body has carried me to where I am today. I need to stop giving it a hard time.

Physical changes of time. I am a young-looking woman for my age (I think) and looking at my mother I can with gratitude put that down to good youthful genes. However, I am feeling the hormones of my youth leaving me. I get very hot. Not so much a sudden hot flush but a gradual overheat. I was always a cold person. Always with a hot water bottle in the winter and sitting close to the radiator.

Last winter I was throwing off my sheets as I was so hot. I get aches, dreadful stomach spasms and cramps, only at night though. My legs and arms ache. Have you ever experienced restless leg syndrome? I get this at night and sometimes in long meetings. Team meetings are a nightmare for me!

I wriggle around for hours. I want to settle but my body does not. I'm suffering from dreadful insomnia. Heart burn is a nightmare, tiredness but I can't sleep because I have terrible insomnia, which actually comes in quite useful for my writing.

I'm struggling to feel I've had enough sleep and when I wake I feel foggy and exhausted. My right arm has torn ligaments, golfer's elbow I believe it's called. I have steroid injections to help at the moment because of all the driving I have to do for my job. It's very difficult for me to be able to rest it. Oh, and I've never been a golfer? I wouldn't mind learning now, it will give me reason for the golfer's elbow.

So, what am I doing to help this? Well one of the first things when I started talking to my coach and mentor was to get a better routine. I have the tiniest gym in the world in my box room, but in here I have a treadmill, a bike and a cross trainer my son gave me. I'm now in there daily if possible for at least half an hour and most days 45 minutes.

I stretch in the morning, to be fair I have little choice in the matter. But the work is paying off. My body looks physically better than it has been for years. I'm a healthy eater. I cook from fresh.

The only thing I don't do is prioritise enough me time. I'm also a rubbish dresser. I will try and change that. I'm not sure how my menopause will go and how long this will last. But I would like to explore better ways of coping with it. I had no idea it would make me feel like this.

I can't take HRT as I have migraines with auras which put me at a higher risk of a stroke. So, I believe the best thing for me is to continue to improve my healthy regime and physical and mental health.

So, what next? Well I decided it was the right time to tell my story because I have got myself into rather desperate situations, which could have got much worse if I hadn't had the strength and resilience to pull myself back on track.

I want to help others like me, to find the best in themselves. Whether it be career wise or personal. I have always tried to be a positive force in people's lives even when I've been in a bad place.

I would like to show you things that I put in place to make things better for me. Health, career, situations that may have happened to you, like me, which have the potential to drag you down. I can only try to explain how I changed my ways.

I did that without being an expert and probably only recently being able to put a lot of these changes I made into words and actually recognise behaviour patterns. I think I have wanted to bring out the best in myself and share what has worked with others. Our strengths, our love, our empathy seems to be what works in many cases.

So, when it comes to how things have improved in my life, I can definitely see the changes I have made in my mind set and wanting to change has been the key. I'm not a top paid executive but shit I'm not a criminal which let's face it, I could have been.

So, did I just grow up? Yes and no. I'm still incredibly childish and see no reason to grow up. I gave up smoking weed as it was doing me no good and I knew it. Like I said it effects each person differently. For me it brought me depression and anxiety. I had to work hard with one of my first counsellors to kick the habit after so long.

I needed to be at my best for the future I wanted. It wasn't a nice experience giving up. I had such terrible stomach cramps and sweats for weeks. But that was only one of the things I did to turn myself around. I have listed a few more things that I think helped.

1/ I started believing in myself

The way I used to think of myself and what I could achieve was not right. I had picked up at an early age from people around me, that I wasn't academic. This was perhaps correct and my dyslexia, even though quite mild was never seen and it was measured on other people's belief.

I was creative and if I would have had someone around who could see where I could excel, I could have achieved better at school. I felt as if I had been written off which carried on in my life for a long time. People had low expectations of me, so I had low expectations of me.

I know now not to believe in others expectations of me but guide myself. I have also learnt to search out similar people who can help me bring out the best in me. That can see me for what I can do and achieve rather than pointing out what I can't.

So, don't let other people's thoughts on you limit your potential.

2/ I learn more and read more I love to learn about new things. For many years now, I have welcomed with open arms learning and reading, to improve my knowledge of things. This year has been a big year for learning. I have had books recommended by my coach which I have devoured and discussed with great excitement in our meetings.

I also love audio books as my job involves a lot of driving around. So, I learn whilst I drive. Also, recommendations from my peers and the people I respect and look up to in business. There is so much to learn out there and it's funny because the older I get I realise the less I actually know, which drives me to learn more. You can learn about anything, just get going and pick up a book which will help, interest, excite and make you grow. I love fiction too and it's great to escape from time to time.

3/Healthy inside and out

We all lead very busy lives. Sometimes it's easy to let your health slip. I had a treadmill in my spare room for a long time and I would get on it sporadically. I now have an exercise bike and cross trainer and this year I have used them 3-4 times a week for 45mins I have made time and now it's become a good habit.

The arm movements on the cross trainer have much improved my arm where my ligaments are torn which means I can go much longer without having a steroid injection. I take care of my skin, as I am always worried about my eczema coming back and I moisturise every day. I cook every day from scratch unless my work takes me away for a few days. I always suffer from that as I get IBS when I'm not controlling my own food.

I need to lose a bit of weight but hey, I'm not in the slightest bit perfect Kate, but I try not to give myself too much of a hard time about that these days.

I do need more time to work on my stress levels, so in the next 12 months I will be looking at ways to learn to relax more. I'm much better than I was, and I used to get stressed much more than I do about work and home.

I just try and put my best effort into everything I can and if that's not good enough I guess there isn't much more I can do. I also try not to get stressed about people's negativity or use of words so much now as usually it's to do with their agenda not mine. Like I mentioned earlier about negativity on social media.

I'm not 100% there with my health but I am learning about what suits me best for my health. I have also found that a bit of Aloe Vera juice helps a lot with my asthma. Found that out by accident whilst using it for IBS, I noticed I had cut back on my asthma inhaler.

4/ I've built a vision and surrounded myself with those who inspire me

This is really important. If you have a vision of something you want to do you need to seek out people who can help you make this vision a reality. It kind of happens naturally once you have a clear vision.

Through my last 12 years I have created visions for myself of things I have wanted to do. I have really been able to see myself doing these things in my mind. You always get people around you that don't visualize in this way so will knock you down, but I have found that if I keep moving towards the goal I have set myself it can become a reality with the right actions.

It does sound a little magical and hippy dippy I know, but it's true. When I had a wobble this year I looked for someone I knew could help me refocus on my vision. For years I have thought about writing a book but not taken it further.

But finding women around me that understood the vision and believed in me.... hey presto I have written a book. If I had not surrounded myself with people who saw that as achievable I may not have done it. The future holds all sorts of things for me and having the right people around me have shown me that at 50 it's not too late for me to start living the best life I can live.

5/I used to get too worked up with things you can't influence

I used to watch loads of news, get worked up by politics and the way things are in the world. Let's be honest, who doesn't? But it went further than that. I had news feeds on my social media and was getting blasted every day.

Also, I would read the comments. It seemed to me that everyone had opposing views and instead of people accepting this, they threw mud at each other. Everyone seems to be an expert in everything these days. I really see the fantastic ways social media can work, but I was getting very down with the constant blasting of media agenda and peoples hate.

I have decided I can't save the whole world, but I can do my bit to help as many people as I can for the rest of my life. I feel so much better moving away from politics and the news. I do still watch a bit, so I know what's going on, but I choose the time and don't allow myself to be controlled by it anymore.

I used to get worked up about decisions made at work or things bosses or line managers said, I don't anymore. If a decision is made above me now and I know it's a given, I don't even waste my energy letting it wind me up. If it's a decision I can influence and am interested in influencing in a positive way, I will put my focus on that. I think I'm just learning not to take things so personally these days and it feels good.

6/I've stopped waiting for others to make me happy

I have spent a lot of my life feeling hurt, angry and wondering when things will get better. One of the best things I have learnt is that I need to find my own happiness. Look for it, be in pursuit of it. I don't mean ridiculous selfish things that will hurt others. I mean my career, my interests. I've met many couples that wait for their partners to change, thinking it will all work out ok.

This is fine, but what if you spend all your life waiting and when it's too late wonder why you didn't take action to make yourself happy and fulfill your dreams. Others can't do that for you, only you can. In some respect I have lowered my expectations of others. Perhaps I had them too high in the past so felt let down by people.

7/ I'm learning to be the best version of me.

I don't want to be anyone else. I want to be me. I've learned to like me. I can always be better though. When I started coaching I told my coach I wanted to be me, but a better me. I may respect and be inspired by others, but I want to be me with my family but better, helping others and working at my best potential. Be yourself but be yourself at your best.

8/ Gratitude

I've learnt the practice of gratitude. I hear a lot of people say this, but I really don't think enough people actually do it. We as humans seem to have a natural ability to be drawn to the negatives in our lives. We look at the things we don't like.

The negative things people have said to us and done to us. I've spent a lot of time with all sorts of negative thoughts in my head bringing me down. If I have an appraisal at work I can be sure to pick up on the one thing I'm doing wrong instead of all the things I'm doing right and generally beat myself for a day or two. Wasted time indeed! I can't get those moments back.

When I first started to look at changing some aspects of my life recently and the way I felt about myself, I was introduced to gratitude. I try each day to think of 3-5 things that I am grateful for.

What I love about this practice is that I have learnt to focus more on the positives. It has been really good for me to refocus my mind to the wonderful people and things going on around me.

Don't get me wrong, I'm human. I still get down, pissed off, feel sorry for myself. But I am able to remind myself of how many great people I know and have known in my life. I'm constantly lucky to meet new people too and I have been lucky in the last few years to make some wonderfully inspiring women who have great belief in me too and are some of my biggest supporters.

I may not want to always work and feel fed up in the mornings, but I do have a great job. I am so grateful that I have pulled myself through dark times. I was able to put food on the table for my family and although I moan about my weight, gaining a little weight during menopause, for now I have my health. So, I can forgive my body for holding on to a few extra pounds.

So with this practice I may look at simple things, like someone where I'm getting my shopping from talking to me and smiling and smiling back. Someone giving way to me when I'm driving. My customers, I do have lovely customers which I'm incredibly grateful for. My children, my husband, my family. I'm grateful I'm not just taken for granted anymore.

Some days can be a real challenge, but I have still found if I can focus my mind on the smaller things I feel grateful for it does really help. This was something I didn't really buy into at first, but I have to admit it's really refocused my mind from just looking for the rubbish things.

There is also something that you can't avoid in life if you want to progress and that's hard work! it doesn't matter how you look at it, because you're never going to get further to get the future you want if you don't work hard at it.

I have been so lucky to have people in my life who I have sought out, who have really pushed me to do better, and most importantly believed in me. I would like to be that person who believes in you. For the times when I have not been able to talk about certain things that have happened to me, let me be the one who you feel you can talk to.

I have come a long way, adoption, health issues, confidence issues, rape, loss and violence, to building myself up in education, career, and now a book. It shows that we can achieve so much. Yes, I'm proud of myself and it's only because I let myself keep thinking one step ahead, dreaming big and not letting those who wrote me off not get to me and keep forging ahead.

My journey is far from finished. I was bought a DNA test by my sons a few Christmas's ago because we still weren't sure on my heritage as it's still not 100% where our family came from. Some said Italian on both sides.

But my DNA came back from all over the world. So, I would like to find out more. The breakdown is below. I would love to find out how they got around so much.

I'm not totally sure how accurate these are, but it was great fun and interesting. I would totally recommend it. Perhaps that's where I got a sense of adventure from? I wonder if there are pirates in our ancestry? It would make a lot of sense .....

Great Britain 54%
West Europe 20%
East Europe 10%
Ireland Scotland and wales 8%
With other smaller % from
Benin/Togo
Scandinavia
Native American
Iberian Peninsula
Nigeria
Finland/Northwest Russia

It seems I am from all over!

I love to listen to women's stories. There is so much we can learn from each other and help each other with. I wish I had got myself a mentor and coach earlier in my life.

It's been fantastic being introduced to a network of women helping each other globally to helping each other to achieve their goals. I write myself off sometimes thinking I'm past it.

But have realised you never are. I would always advise other women to get a mentor or coach. Those who have seen my journey over the last 12 months would agree my focus has changed and my possibility about myself and future has grown. Your never past it or over the hill.

Is the menopause going to get the better of me? Hell no!! Like millions of other women, I will find a way of getting through this. After all it's just another challenge.

28 Lucky

It's a strange thing to start writing a book on my life story. I don't really think my life has been anything out of the ordinary. I speak to friends and they want to hear about the things I have done. They gasp and laugh as I am just me. Their mate, colleague, mother, wife.

To me the interesting thing is possibly my motivations. What made me do things that were not the sort of thing someone like me would do? There may be times in this book you think "How the hell did you get to that point?" I wonder these things myself.

I have been worried about talking about myself and my life. I've felt apologetic and thought I should hide it from people. What if people change their views about me, what if I lose my job, my livelihood and actually push myself back to where I was in my darker days?

I do understand that if I hadn't have told my story as honestly as possible, I wouldn't be in a position to help others turn themselves around and I realise that the negativity I have experienced in the end hasn't defined my whole character, in the I can turn these experiences into positives.

It's as if part of the tests in my life have meant I have had to endure certain things in order to find my path, my meaning, my why. I'm not advising anyone follows my path into negativity, I'm just saying that this was part of my journey.

We all have paths we can walk down and doors we can open. It's just a matter of choice's we make. I admit I made some bad choices, I also had some bad ones made for me. Perhaps you will all tut and judge me.

Perhaps you will say I turned things around. I don't know, but let's just start by saying, all those who I mention I feel great love for. Even those who wronged me. In life I've realised that hate only grows as bitterness in your heart which will only hurt.

I have been very lucky to have had the love in my life to draw from to gain strength. My goal is to be that support and hand to hold for those who are not lucky enough to have that...yet.

For all those alive in my memories, please don't feel angry at your mention. You have all gone on to have good lives with love and for that I'm truly glad. I would not wish to hurt anyone, just help those who may share similar experience.

I have been blessed with amazing family. Two sets of parents!!! That's unusual indeed and 3 fantastic children.

A husband who has to deal with my restlessness. I'm sure we will find more happiness as we grow in life. A brother who can always make me laugh and sisters I don't know enough yet. To all of you this may be shocking, and you may be cross I've put this out there. But let's all work together to make a better place for us and those we can help. I'm so proud of you all.

To my kids. I'm constantly amazed how you've grown, you are talented, good and loving. I'm always happy you survived my bringing you up.... And also, to the boys your memories of childhood were good. My beautiful daughter is lucky to have such good big brothers. She got the best of me as a mum I think.

Hopefully we can create a positive legacy.

I have been written off by many time and time again. I have been very close at times to writing myself off. But my strength had always come through. If someone tells you that you can't do something, remember young Kates saying

"I will if you won't Let me !!"

29 Update

I thought this would be a good thing to add right at the end. Although this book had been in my mind for many years, the process really started after booking a family trip to Rhodes, Greece, 33 years after I was raped there. I had booked the holiday and actually realised after, the feelings this trip may bring back. It did feel like a bit of a test for me.

It was thirty-three years ago when I last was in Rhodes. I was happy to go back. I knew I was over what had happened on my last visit there. I booked a family hotel just outside Faliraki, had a lovely week of relaxation there with my husband and daughter. We swam, sunbathed, read, ate and drank.

I booked two-day trips, One to Turkey on the Sunday and an island boat trip which would take us on a couple of swim locations heading in to Lindos as the last stop with a thee hour stop time so we could have a look around.

The boat trip was lovely. We stopped at Anthony Quinn bay where my daughter swam in the clear waters, then we headed on to Lindos. As the boat made its way round, I could see the Acropolis and marvelled at its beauty. The first thought that came to mind was my mum. I thought how when I last visited Lindos it was the last holiday I had with her. I can remember her standing up in the Acropolis with a white cotton tee shirt and a black striped skirt. She used to wear some silly white brimmed sunglasses, in my mind she was wearing those.

As the boat moored, I could see at the far side of the beach where the road winded down and where the incident happened 33 years ago. But my mind instantly then moved on to how beautiful the little houses were and imagining the one we stayed at with a brown wooden door, a cooling courtyard where my mum and dad and their friends would sit and chat and read their books.

We got off the boat and walked around the village. It was very hot and packed with tourists. A lot busier than it was when I was last there. I remembered the donkeys and how we had taken one up to the Acropolis and how we wouldn't have got on a donkey today, my Mum would have been sad to see them now. She loved donkeys and would tell me how they got their cross on their backs from Jesus choosing a donkey to ride into Jerusalem.

I remembered my friend who was with me all those years ago and the absolute laughs we used to have when we holidayed together. I used to love our holidays. We were such good friends.

I didn't get around to St Pauls Bay where we stayed, but we went for some food on Pallas beach and swam in the sea. I made a mental note that I would return to Lindos again and stop in a villa with a cool courtyard and read and relax.

One thing that didn't matter anymore is what happened there on my last visit as the boat pulled away it was my mum I saw again. She had guided me around and made me see the place for its full beauty. It was the last holiday I had with her, she was still there for me. It was her memory here that was the strongest, not the rape.

Lindos is a beautiful place, I feel totally at ease with it now and will be back. What happened to me there was the actions of one person, it really had very little to do with me or the place. It was the right thing for me to go back to see that. I think the healing is complete.

ABOUT THE AUTHOR

Kate Blake Lives in Smethwick in the West Midlands Where she has lived for most of her life. She lives with her husband, daughter and dog Jade. Her sons live locally in Birmingham with their partners.

If you want to contact her about Coaching, you can contact her on

info@kate-blake.com

www.kate-blake.com

Printed in Poland
by Amazon Fulfillment
Poland Sp. z o.o., Wrocław